OCEANS OF BIRDS

OCEANS OF BIRDS

TONY SOPER

Illustrations by Michael Loates

DAVID & CHARLES
Newton Abbot   London

British Library Cataloguing in Publication Data

Soper, Tony
  Oceans of birds.
  1. Marine birds
  I. Title
598.29'24

ISBN 0-7153-9199-2

Typeset and designed on a Macintosh system
by John Youé
and printed in West Germany by Mohndruck GmBH
for David & Charles Publishers plc
Brunel House Newton Abbot Devon

CONTENTS

LIST OF ILLUSTRATIONS

INTRODUCTION

Small boats are ideal for birdwatching in inshore waters, big ships for ocean wanderers. But any kind of vessel offers the great bonus that birds seem almost indifferent to their passage, provided they proceed at a civilised speed and with proper respect. Try getting close to shorebirds from the land and they won't tolerate it, but they let a canoe or a dinghy pass comfortably close. Graduate to a ferry or a cruise-ship and the birds positively seek you out as a welcome source of food.

Ever since I learnt to handle a heavy pulling-boat in the Cattewater and ventured into Plymouth Sound, I have delighted in finding birds at sea. Through the years I have enjoyed the experience from an assortment of vessels, sometimes as skipper, sometimes as crew or passenger and more recently – with my wife – as a sort of birdwatcher's nanny. First we shepherded parties in search of the elegant Avocets on the Tamar estuary in south-west England. Then with the 2,500 ton *Lindblad Explorer* we cruised the Indian Ocean, learning how to cope with the demands of a hundred enthusiastic American birders; taking Zodiac-loads of twelve senior citizens and introducing them, on their first-ever dives, to the delights of snorkelling in the shark-infested coral inlets of Aldabra; tracking Roseate Terns on the white sand beaches of the Seychelles and hunting the Black Paradise Fly-catcher. Later, with different vessels of the splendid P&O fleet, we led parties in the Norwegian Sea to the North Cape seeing the

White-tailed Sea Eagle; to the Baltic for Velvet (White-winged) Scoters and the Mediterranean for Eleanora's Falcon and Audouin's Gull.

I reached down to the Falkland Islands in the South Atlantic with the RAF and the Galapagos Islands in the Pacific with the Ecuadorean Navy. But the greatest thrill of all for a sea-going birder was the chance to sail round the world with the mighty and beautiful steamship *Canberra*. My seven-year-old son Jack found Cassin's Auklet in the swimming pool one morning before breakfast. We watched albatrosses power-glide down the wake to join us, we sailed through a sea of shearwaters inside the Great Barrier Reef of Australia and rescued some from a sticky end (becoming curry for the Goanese seamen). We gave over our bathroom to a succession of dazed terns and petrels which came to grief on the decks at night and needed peace and quiet. We even learnt to grin and bear it when the loudspeaker system called us to duty with the announcement, so much appreciated by the passengers, 'There is a bird in Tony Soper's cabin'. One of the greatest pleasures of the trip was the discovery that almost everybody on the ship became genuinely interested in the seabirds which passed by and the landbirds which occasionally joined the ship for a rest and some biscuit crumbs.

Wherever we went on board there was someone who was looking at a distant bird or wanted to tell of one he'd seen during the day. There was the old boy who stretched out in his favourite deck-chair round about teatime, on the promenade deck, togged out in his dinner jacket and black tie, and ready to chatter about boobies and storm-petrels. While we practised our hymns in the ad-hoc church choir I would sneak a look through the porthole to watch for passing birds. While we stretched out on the games deck, doing our daily dozen, the frigatebirds would soar overhead, doubtless sizing us up as possible breakfasts and thinking better of it. And, best of all, at drinks time in the evening we would lean on a rail with the stalwart band of birdwatchers who girdled the world with us, discussing the day's bird list and admiring the shearwaters as they slanted and turned as we scanned the horizon for whales and the sky for tropicbirds. It was a mind-boggling experience.

In those hundred days we chalked up a list of six hundred and

Tony Soper with two Black Noddies which hitched a lift off the Queensland coast inside the Great Barrier Reef
ELIZABETH WATTS

fifty species. But since there are less than three hundred different kinds of seabird in the world and we didn't see anywhere near all of them, our list was bolstered by a lot of birds which we saw at our ports of call. We became experts in planning to get twenty-four hours of birding into an eight-hour stopover. And I've included some of our lists, in the order in which we saw our birds, warts and all, just because I hope they may be encouraging to others who, perforce, may have no more than one day in Acapulco or Honolulu or Auckland or Colombo and wonder what they might see. Given two days in Sydney, you cannot fail to collect a cornucopia of birds.

But for the major sections of the classic round-the-world cruise, and the typical North Sea, Mediterranean, Alaskan and South Atlantic voyages, I have tried to indicate the way that the bird panorama unfolds. It is broadly true that you can predict the way in which new species will appear, coast by coast and sea by sea. The pre-ordained sequence of events is one of the great pleasures of the journey – one day out of San Francisco, watch for the Laysan

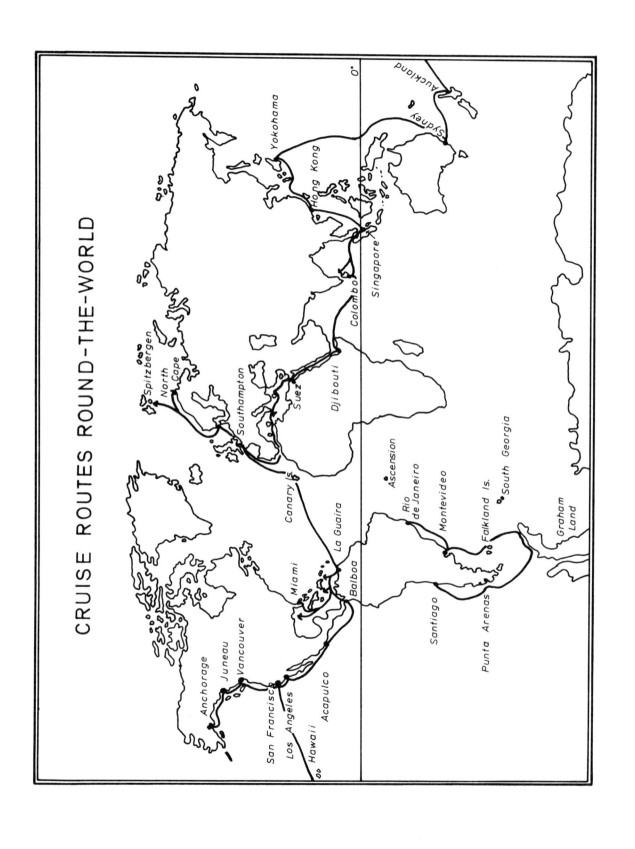

CRUISE ROUTES ROUND-THE-WORLD

Albatross; approaching Australia offers your best chance of the mighty Wandering Albatross.

Seventy-one per cent of our planet's surface is covered by water, 139 million square miles of it. For every square mile of land there are two and a half of sea. Much of that watery expanse is unknown and unexplored. Yet ocean-going birds have the freedom of those seas and wander them in numbers that stun the imagination. One of the tiny water-walking storm-petrels may be the commonest bird in the world even though penguin cities number their inhabitants in the tens of millions. Albatrosses spend most of their lives soaring the stormy latitudes of the roaring forties, circling the entire Antarctic continent. The sea-swallows have cracked the problem of winter by criss-crossing the globe and flying through a life of endless summer.

If we choose to follow such birds, we can share something of the romance of their lives. Naval seamen, merchant seamen, weathership crews, cruise-ships and their passengers, yachtsmen and all, have a chance of seeing something of these other world travellers. For one of the enjoyable traits of pelagic birds is that they seem to seek out ships and pay them a visit, sometimes brief, sometimes prolonged. Any voyage is enhanced by a small understanding of these travelling companions.

It has to be said that, apart from the birds which actually come aboard and hitch a lift, a lot of them will be rather distant and difficult to identify. Take your eyes off the dipping wings for one moment and they have a disconcerting tendency to disappear behind a wave, for good. So you certainly need to concentrate, to scan the sea from alongside to the far horizon and into the sky. There will be birdless days in the open ocean but plenty of others when, after logging a few dozen excitements, a passing jogger on the prom deck will commiserate with you, saying, 'Not a bird in sight today!', because of course they haven't been looking. Worse still, on days when you're hugging the coast they will say, 'Bad luck, nothing but seagulls today', as if gulls were small change rather than fearsome challenges of identification.

There are no hard-and-fast rules about where to watch from on a ship, since birds can appear at any time almost anywhere. But the afterdeck is as good a place as any, for many birds like to watch a ship's wake for galley waste or for the marine organisms

Opposite:
Round-the-world cruises

11

*Fishing-boats, whether
engaged in inshore or
distant water activities,
provide rich opportunities
for gulls, petrels and
gannets. But commercial
fishing represents
significant competition for
fish stocks*
W. WISNIEWSKI/FLPA

churned up by the propellors. For fishing boobies the foredeck is ideal, for whale-watching you must get yourself as close to the bridge-wings as possible with a forward view. But for every bird seen best from the foreparts of the ship, there's another at the stern, so you must hedge your bets and do some patrolling.

A moderate speed of up to 10 knots is ideal for birding, but it's no good telling that to the master of a cruise-liner, or a cross-channel ferry for that matter. On the other hand albatrosses have to make endless sweeps and turns just to reduce speed to keep station at well over 20 knots. And I was overtaken by a couple of razorbills while screaming along in a hydrofoil off the coast of Brittany at 36 knots.

Migrating landbirds sometimes find a great deal of difficulty in landing on a vessel which is steaming fast; they certainly prefer a stationary ship, for example a weathership or an oil platform, especially at night. They are usually exhausted and simply looking for a rest. Seabirds are attracted to ships for different reasons: they provide some shelter in a lee; a roost-place; or most of all because they provide food in the form of the galley waste of which most ships are regrettably prodigal.

This book seeks to provide a simple introduction to some of the possibilities of seabird-watching at sea. It is in no sense exhaustive. Its object is to pave the way for a more wholehearted appreciation of the pleasures of ocean-going birdwatching. It is not an identification manual, since that function is already well and truly served by Peter Harrison's book *Seabirds: An Identification Guide,* a volume which should be in every bird-cruiser's cabin. Because of the labyrinthine confusion of English seabird names (your Blue-eyed Shag is another man's King Cormorant and everyone else's Imperial Shag), I have gratefully plumped for Harrison's expertise and the English names in this book follow his standardisation. Please use the index to resolve the sort of problems I have just hinted at, and you will find that the Slender-billed Shearwater reveals itself in this book as Short-tailed. Fortunately, the British List is at present in the throes of revision by the Records Committee of the British Ornithologists Union, and about time too, for the Australians and the Americans have led the way.

Seabirds have suffered greatly in the past from man's greed and indifference to their suffering. Masters of the seas they may be, but when they come ashore to breed they are often clumsy and at a disadvantage. Their eggs and chicks have been exploited mercilessly through the centuries, and only recently have we begun to give them the consideration they so richly deserve in the form of protection by law. Sadly, as public opinion warmed in their favour, first oil pollution claimed many of their lives, now the insidious menace of chemical and nuclear waste is even more horrific. Multinational fisheries compete with seabirds for their prey on unequal terms. Man-made debris litters the oceans, fishing-nets trap auks, fishing-net fragments strangle gannets. International law forbids the disposal of waste at sea, but the policemen are few and far between.

As seabirds are mostly out of sight it is easy to put them out of mind. It is so important for those of us who care to join the right societies and support their work (addresses on p200).

And don't tell yourself you'll never see these wonderful birds at sea because you can't afford the cruise-ticket, for there's more than one way... One of my long-time friends decided twenty years ago that he wanted to see the world's birds. He couldn't afford to do it the easy way so he signed on as a steward in a procession of varied vessels from coasters to the grandest liners. So he has travelled the seven seas and seen all the birds in every port!

GENERAL SURFACE CURRENTS AND UPWELLINGS

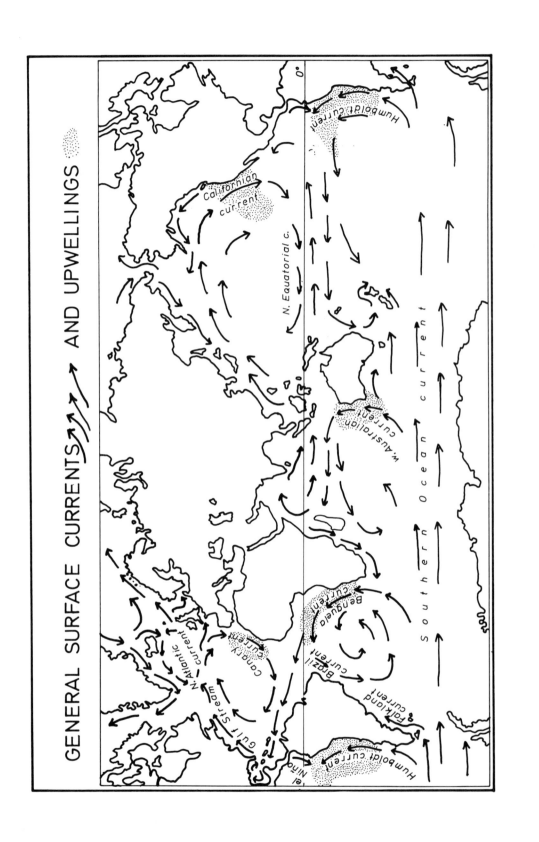

LIFE
ON THE OCEAN
WAVE

W e know that many millions of seabirds live there, yet on rare days of glassy calm the sea looks featureless, flat and lifeless to a casual observer. On wild wet and frightening days it may still seem superficially barren. But appearances are deceptive, and the winds which whip the surface into such varied responses also power the currents which are the key to unlock a cornucopian abundance of food supporting unimaginable numbers of birds.

At first sight it seems eccentric behaviour for a bird to commit its life to these empty wastes but there is, of course, method in the madness. Provided they can learn to live with some demanding requirements, there is a good living to be made at sea.

The sea's bounty is unleashed by the driving forces of climate, wind and the Earth's rotation. Although it can be quirky and variable in association with land masses, at sea the wind's force is remarkably persistent and stable over vast areas. On either side of the Equatorial Trough – more popularly known as the doldrums – are the reliable trade winds, blowing an average moderate breeze (force 4) northeasterly in the Northern and southeasterly in the Southern Hemisphere. In the East Atlantic, the northern part of the Indian Ocean, the western part of the North Pacific and Northern Australia they are replaced by monsoons which are characterised by seasonal reversals of wind and weather systems. Powered by the constant factor of the Earth's spin, the winds

Opposite:
Circulating currents bring mineral-rich cold water from the poles to the surface in areas of upwelling. Because these waters sustain huge quantities of plankton life these are the areas where seabirds are most abundant

Opposite:
The classic 'food chain', in which mineral-rich upwellings fuel microscopic plant growth – Phytoplankton *– which is in turn grazed by the* Zooplankton *whose tiny animals are prey for larger and yet larger animals which themselves return nutrients in the form of excrement through their livers and their bodies when they die. This chain gives a highly simplified picture. Some very large animals, like the Basking Shark or the Humpback Whale, short-circuit the system by feeding directly on the plankton animals*

Overleaf:
Vast numbers of seabirds congregate off the coast of Peru and Chile where the Humboldt Current upwells to provide a feast of anchovies for Inca, Sandwich and Elegant Terns, Band-tailed and Franklin's Gulls and Olivaceous Cormorants
LEO BATTEN/FLPA

create currents which are, in turn, affected by the character of the ocean floor and the land masses with their associated shallow-water shelves.

Currents are created mainly by the direct action of wind on the sea, when frictional drag pulls the surface water in its direction, and they are therefore generally stronger at the surface. In both the South Atlantic and the Pacific the trade winds drag an immense band of water eastwards over some 50° of latitude, revolving round the polar continent and balanced by a much narrower belt of west-going counter-current at the equator. The global effect is of continuous circulations in the great oceans, clockwise in the Northern and anti-clockwise in the Southern Hemisphere.

Currents are complex and monstrous in their capacity. In the North Atlantic, the Gulf Stream carries an astonishing six and a half million cubic yards of warm water per second. As it moves to the surface on its northward journey it cools and sinks, returning southwards at depth. And the effect of the currents, from the point of view of all life in and above the sea, is crucial. For where currents meet, or where they are faced with immovable objects like islands or land masses, there are areas of turbulence. And it is in these confused waters that food is most plentiful, as a direct result of the mineral nutrients carried by the movement of waters. Where cold deep water rises to the surface to replace water driven from a coast by persistent winds it brings nitrates and phosphates harvested from distant seabeds; these nutrient salts are characteristic of the upwellings which generate life-forms in unimaginable numbers.

The food available to sustain sea-going birds relates in quantity indirectly to the concentrations of nutrients in upwelling waters. For these nutrients, along with the power of the sun's light and warmth and the saltiness of the sea are the raw materials which are taken up by microscopic plants like diatoms in the free-floating *Phytoplankton*. In turn the surface 'meadows' of plankton plants are 'grazed' by copepods and a myriad of other plankton animals of the *Zooplankton*. And these tiny morsels are in turn hunted by larger invertebrates and by fish. And in their turn those crustaceans and molluscs and fish are hunted by larger fish and by birds, seals, whales and man. In the course of time those 'higher'

animals return, to the sea, a generous proportion of their food as excrement and at the last they bequeath their bodies to decay and sink to the bottom to be scavenged and to provide basic nutrients all over again in a merry-go-round of life-forces.

There are seasonal forces at work in fuelling the sea's bounty. In springtime, when the sun is climbing higher and the strength of its light is increasing and providing energy, the plant plankton blooms, thrives and multiplies. Single-celled plants divide and double themselves in a day; within a couple of weeks the original has given rise to astronomic progeny. The microscopic free-floating animals have not been idle, either, and grazing on the lush pastures they flourish mightily by the summer, by which time the plants are having a rest. A second, lesser, bloom in the autumn allows the animals a chance to fatten themselves before winter comes to test them with lean times.

These bloomings are of course not evenly distributed over the oceans. In the tropics relatively stable conditions of temperature and light create uniformly warm conditions; coupled with light and variable winds, the sea is not overly productive. Uncluttered with plankton the calm waters appear a sterile blue. Whereas in the roaring forties of the southern ocean the wild sea is loaded with life and shows the bright green of a pasture.

Coastal waters offer sustenance to large numbers of birds because not only is there a great deal of turbulence in the shallow sea but because debouching river water brings yet another mixture of nutrients. There are always more birds per average square mile in inshore waters than there are far out at sea.

Sometimes an upwelling current fails, as for instance when a contrary wind temporarily reverses the flow and replaces cold rich water with warm lean water. When the Humboldt Current fails to bring its mineral riches to the coast of South America, disaster threatens the vast congregations of guano birds off the coast of Chile and Peru. When the warm El Niño current penetrates too far south and displaces the plankton-rich Humboldt from the coast, the vast shoals of anchovies which come inshore to feed on the plankton move away as well. And the Guanay Cormorants, Peruvian Pelicans and Boobies suffer catastrophic losses. The population may fall from twenty million to one million in a season. The result is bad news for both fishermen and fisher-birds which are denied the anchovies, and for the industry which harvests the birds' excrement as guano for the fertiliser trade. Although the historic deposits of guano were worked out by the end of the nineteenth century, even the year-by-year bounty deposited by the birds represents a substantial resource. In the early sixties the eighteen million guano birds of the Peruvian Chinchas Islands produced the staggering quantity of 180,000 tons of nitrogen-rich fertiliser every year. But the continued production was inevitably affected by direct competition at sea between the anchovy fishermen and the birds seeking the same prey. Off the coast of south-west Africa, incidentally, artificial platforms have been constructed to encourage the Cape Gannets to nest and provide guano for convenient harvesting, an arrangement of mutual benefit to both birds and man.

The seas of the world are an interconnected, continuous system, but nevertheless they contain variations of habitat which result from differences in temperature, salinity, depth and currents. These create barriers to movement just as effectively as deserts or mountain ranges separate animal populations ashore. Penguins are confined to the Southern Hemisphere because the tropical warm-water belt of the equator offers no food to sustain them. Albatrosses are confined to their natal hemisphere because the calm air of the doldrums offers no lift for them to glide across.

Tropical oceans maintain the lowest level of food production, so although a greater variety of seabird species may be recorded there, you must go to the polar regions if you want to see sheer numbers of birds. However, there are fewer species which have been able to adapt to the demanding conditions in high latitudes. And most seabirds only visit the polar and subpolar regions at their summer times of great abundance. The windy latitudes of the roaring forties of the Antarctic Convergence between 40^0 and 60^0 South are the richest in the shrimp-like krill *Euphausia superba* in the brief summer. The sea is awash with krill, they multiply to staggering numbers and are carried north by the currents, to be eaten by equally staggering numbers of birds; penguins, prions, shearwaters and petrels, to say nothing of whales.

On land it is the border zone between woodland and pasture which sees the greatest bird activity. So it is at sea, where two currents meet or an upwelling disturbs surface calm, that you find seabirds feeding on the surface fish and invertebrates in this 'edge country'.

One other, relatively minor phenomenon, may often appear in calm water to puzzle an observer. When a wind blows constantly in one direction it sets up minor surface currents in that direction. They in turn produce helical air-current vortices which cause two surface layers of water to flow towards each other and sink. In these convergence lines, which lie more or less parallel to the wind, flotsam and organic slicks, called 'Langmuir's Windrows', are often marked by a 'tide-line' of floating weed, plankton organisms and odds and ends. These windrows attract scavengers, from albatrosses to storm-petrels.

So one way and another there are vast quantities of food in the sea, and clearly that is what has encouraged birds to exploit the marine environment. But the sea is a hard place to live and birds must be superbly adapted to an unusual lifestyle. Some are deep-sea sailors, like albatrosses and shearwaters; some are inshore fishermen and longshoremen, like cormorants and most of the gulls. Some, like divers (loons) and grebes, spend only part of the year at sea; some, like sea-ducks, specialise in shallow-water diving. But seabirds are not as diverse a group as those of the land, for of roughly nine thousand kinds of birds less than three hundred can be called seabirds.

The truly pelagic (ocean-going) birds must learn to cope with a vast open ocean. There is nowhere to perch but on the heaving waves (or an occasional piece of driftwood or a ship). They must be able to endure both oily calms and violent storms when there are towering waves, no place of shelter and stinging salt spray in their faces. They may have to endure temperatures ranging from tropical heat to polar cold. But they manage with ease.

Birds make subtle use of the varying wind draughts associated with waves. They ride the updraught created as wind presses against waves. They can rise above the crest, then soar along the trough using complex energy-differences set up by the friction between the opposing forces of wind and water. In this way they ride the endless waves. And by the same token they will ride the bow and quarter waves set up by the passage of a displacement vessel through the sea. They tend to drift with a wind, as do, for instance, the birds of the southern ocean who work the never still

westerlies and revolve around the Antarctic continent.

In times of violent weather seabirds will avoid the worst of it if possible. They survive hurricanes by getting out of their way. Provided there's plenty of sea room they simply drift to leeward out of the path of the cyclone, returning to station when the worst is past. In just plain gales they will avoid the worst effects by riding them out in the lee of a wave, flying along in parallel and on the sheltered side. For all that, disaster does strike, especially in the case of the smaller and lighter species. Phalaropes are especially vulnerable; attempting to ride it out on the surface they may be simply blown into the air. Huge numbers die in storms. Little Auks and storm-petrels may be 'wrecked' ashore in great numbers in inclement weather, to be discovered wandering disconsolately around the rain-sodden streets of inland towns where they are absurdly out of place.

On the plus side, the great virtue of the sea is that it is a relatively safe place most of the time. There are no foxes and very few people.

Albatrosses are masters of soaring flight. The Laysan Albatrosses breed in the Hawaiian Islands but range far over the North Pacific
TONY SOPER

25

An insignificant number of penguins are taken by Leopard Seals; food shortage or failure is a much more effective control on numbers. But seabirds carry reserves of fat and certainly the larger species can endure long periods of starvation. In storms, plankton-feeders like the smaller auks may suffer because the surface plankton migrates downwards away from the turbulence. Fishing activities by man, however, pose a very real threat to seabirds in some areas. Twenty thousand auks drown in trammel nets in Galway Bay alone each year. The Greenland drift nets are said to deal with a half a million guillemots annually. Discarded pieces of net may be picked up and taken ashore as nesting material, to trap legs and strangle the necks of gannets.

A bird's secret weapon is its feathers, the invention which allowed them to spread and thrive all over the planet. Feathers not only keep them warm and provide opportunities for colourful display, they give the power to fly economically, to escape from enemies and to explore food and breeding opportunities wherever they may be. But feathers are subject to wear and tear, and to the ageing effects of the ultra-violet rays in sunlight, so there has to be a continual programme of maintenance and periodic replace-ment. You may often see birds scratching their heads in flight, or indulging in hair-raising preening acrobatics when they are alone, or sometimes while they glide downwind. But they choose the time and the place for their seasonal moults with care.

Wing shapes vary enormously amongst birds, but many of the ocean-going seabirds have typically long and narrow wings, as in fulmars and albatrosses, for instance. They are gliders, made for effortless soaring, making use of thermals or the lift from wave-winds. Shearwaters have long narrow wings, too, but they are more flexible than those of albatrosses, and they are able to 'fly' underwater to a certain extent. Auks have short narrow wings and fly in air with difficulty and underwater with great skill. Penguins are master submariners, with even shorter wings,they cannot fly at all.

Typically, seabirds have webbed feet, though in the case of the phalaropes they are almost non-existent. Storm-petrels walk on the sea with them, cormorants use them as propulsion units in diving and active pursuit of prey. In many species they are useful not only in assisting water-borne take-offs but as brakes and control surfaces in seemingly difficult aerial manoeuvres.

Classic experiments have confirmed that seabirds are well able to find their way about the unmarked oceans. When Ronald Lockley had Manx Shearwaters flown by aeroplane to Rio de Janeiro, they returned to their nest-burrow on Skokholm Island off the coast of Wales in sixteen days, averaging 460 miles (740km) per day. In the case of a Laysan Albatross, it returned 3,200 miles (5,150km) to its nest in ten days.

In coasting along inshore waters, seabirds use the visual signals of cliffs, headlands, 'conspic houses' and doubtless lighthouses too, just as sailors do. And in making journeys out of sight of land, they navigate just as seamen do, by observing heavenly bodies and measuring time by their highly efficient biological clocks. They are perfectly capable of setting a course and measuring distance run. They use a variety of senses in gathering information. The sounds of waves, distant echoes from far-off cliffs and mountains, even smell, in the case of tube-nosed species, as we shall see later. And they are able to sense the Earth's magnetic field, so even have an inbuilt compass, with magnetite in their nervous system. In a magnetic storm they become disoriented, exactly as one would expect.

What seems most likely is that birds have access to a whole range of navigational aids and that they make use of them according to the weather conditions and problems they face at any particular time. The only certain thing is that the systems work, except on the occasions when foul weather deprives them of stimulus.

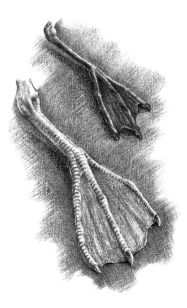

The webbed feet of a storm-petrel are much smaller than those of a fulmar, but both have claws on the toes. Although they are poorly equipped for walking on land, when the claws may be useful in rock-climbing, they are well able to walk on water

Cormorants

Double-crested
Olivaceous
Little Black
Great
Indian
Cape
Socotra
Bank
Japanese
Brandt's
Shag
Pelagic
Red-faced
Rock Shag

Guanay
Pied
Black-faced
New Zealand King
Campbell Island
Imperial
Red-legged Shag
Spotted Shag
Little Pied
Long-tailed
Crowned
Javanese
Pygmy
Galapagos

Cormorants are widely distributed round the world, though not in parts of northern Asia, Canada and the central Pacific. Most of the twenty-eight species live in the Southern Hemisphere, where, for some reason, they tend to have whiter underparts. The family includes both cormorants and shags, whose names and identification cause a great deal of confusion. Taxonomically speaking, they are all cormorants. The word cormorant derives from the Latin *corvus marinus* or the French *cor marin,* but either way it is certainly a sea crow. The size of the bird, its colour and its rounded wings all bear a resemblance to crows. Shag is an Olde English word for 'tuft', and the breeding crest on the British shag certainly fits the description.

Cormorants are medium to large birds, with long necks, longish wings, a stiff wedge-tail, slender, cylindrical bills with a sharp hook and strong legs, placed well aft to act as a powerful twin-paddle propulsion unit. The plumage is usually black in the adult, with a purple or green metallic sheen, sometimes white underparts. Usually there is a bare but brightly coloured patch around the face.

They are coastal birds, rarely out of sight of land, some frequent inland waters. Goose-like in flight, they are more loon (diver)-like in the water, where they float deeply, with little freeboard. Slow-moving fish and crustaceans are their main food. Eels are taken in large numbers. Their technique is to swim-dive and chase underwater. Jack-knifing from the surface, they spring a little into the air and dive head first. The paddle-feet give propulsion, the wings act as control surfaces. They work mostly in shallow water, but can dive to 15 fathoms if necessary. Most dive sessions last less than a minute.

The Guanay Cormorants of the Humboldt Current area locate shoals while they are flying, then swoop down and dive, they are operating in clear water and can see their prey. But cormorants can locate prey without difficulty in murky water with poor visibility. Both the Guanay and the North American Double-crested Cormorant also fish co-operatively, driving schools of fish to concentrate them.

Cormorant plumage is markedly unwaterproof, the contour feathers are modified to allow air out and water in when underwater, an adaptation well suited to diving birds. Also their bones are less pneumatic and they have no air sacs under the skin, the character which makes gannets, boobies and pelicans so buoyant. They also swallow pebbles for ballast and possibly to adjust their trim. These facilities serve the bird well underwater, but after a fishing session it has only a sluggish flight capability and must ventilate its wings to dry them, thus accounting for the umbrella stance which they adopt while standing on a convenient post drying their sails.

The catch is brought to the surface to swallow, behaviour which led to their domestication by wily fishermen. Tethered to a bow-perch by lines attached to leather collars round their necks, the team of birds brought their catch back to their owner because they were unable to swallow them. This method of fishing was perfected by the Japanese, who still demonstrate their skills for the tourists.

Cormorants are much persecuted wherever fishermen perceive them as overly successful competitors (ie anywhere that men and cormorants occur together). But in reality their catch is non-commercial. Where fish are provided in unnatural superabundance, for instance at fish farms, the cormorants inevitably take their tithe, but this does not prove that trout and salmon are their everyday fare.

In breeding, cormorants are socially inclined, their colonies, on cliff slopes, ledges or in bushes and trees, may be very large. They blossom into ornamental plumage at the onset of breeding, with crests, wing and thigh bars or odd-coloured plumes. The nest is of sticks or seaweed or guano, often decorated with freshly picked flowers or some trifle collected on the beach. They breed in their third or fourth year, lay from two to six eggs which are incubated by the

warm-blooded webs on the feet, since they have no brood patch (gannets and boobies use the same method).

The quantity of nitrogen-rich guano (excrement) they produce can be so impressive that it becomes a commercial proposition to market it as fertiliser. The Cape Cormorant of South Africa and the Guanay Cormorant of Peru both contribute significantly to their nation's economies.

One last, and most curious, cormorant lives only on the Galapagos Islands. The Galapagos Cormorant is flightless, having given up flight a very long time ago. Its flight muscle is much reduced and it has no keel on its sternum, its wings have shrunk to operate only as flippers, in penguin style. It is markedly tame and indifferent to man, another characteristic of island isolation. The small and vulnerable population needs sympathetic protection.

DESIGN FOR
FISHING

Birds have developed a remarkable range of fishing methods in order to carve up amongst themselves the various dishes on offer. Some specialise in picking off tiny plankton items at their leisure, some chase high-speed fish, some are scavengers, some are general-purpose opportunists and some are thieves, taking food from other birds. Outside the breeding season, when they are released from the responsibility of taking a catch back to the nest ashore, they tend to be nomadic, sometimes travelling great distances in search of food.

Few landbirds have developed their sense of smell, for they don't need it. But at sea it can have real value when, for instance, a floating whale corpse may be surrounded by hundreds of miles of featureless ocean. Tube-nosed birds are able to sniff it out from a great distance and flock to the feast. Giant Petrels, especially, excel at this useful task which tidies the ocean.

In albatrosses and fulmars, for example, the nostrils extend as tubes along the bill, and the nasal chambers house a complex organ which includes valvular structures which may act as anemometers so that the bird is able to measure air pressure, a useful facility in dynamic soaring. But the nose is also an organ of smell, a particularly useful sense for scavengers. The tube-noses represent a highly successful sea-going group of birds, including albatrosses, shearwaters, petrels and storm-petrels. (Wilson's Storm-

Petrel *may* be the world's most abundant bird.) Ocean-going mariners, in both blue and green water, they spend their entire lives at sea except for the enforced breeding period at some remote island. All have webbed feet, with no hind toe, and they carry with them a powerful musky odour caused by the stomach oil which they will so freely spout at you if alarmed. Most of them breed in the Southern Hemisphere, some migrate north to 'winter' in the northern summer. And, likewise, those which breed in that northern summer, like the Manx Shearwater, fly south to 'winter' in the southern summer, thus making maximum use of the different seasons of plenty.

Those which breed in tropical and sub-tropical latitudes tend to be more sedentary, because seasonal differences in those latitudes are less marked. Many of them are confirmed ship-followers and they are keen on galley waste. They are most enthusiastic in pursuit of whaling and fishing vessels since these can provide a significant source of high-calorie offal. In much the same way as freely available garden bird-table food sustains many first-winter passerines through to their first summer, so many first-year seabirds must bless the wasteful habits of ships.

Seabirds' bills: top left, *auk;* top right, *petrel;* below left, *shearwater;* bottom right, *tern*

31

Seabirds live more or less exclusively on animal matter, from *Zooplankton* to fish, but they have evolved an armoury of methods for hunting it. Albatrosses and shearwaters may duck under the surface and peck, or pluck from the surface in flight. Diving-petrels whir along at zero feet and plunge into the waves after shrimps and small fish. Storm-petrels feed on the wing, feet dangling and 'walking' on the water, sucking oily food from the surface.

White Pelicans fish co-operatively, line abreast (a form of pair-trawling) advancing on a shoal with their great beaks scooping in the water. Brown Pelicans have a much more spectacular technique, diving from a height in active chase of individual fish. This 'plunge-diving' is characteristic of the widespread family group of gannets and boobies. Typically they will be spread out over the sea at a distance from each other until one of the party locates a shoal. In plunging into the sea, the tell-tale flash of white alerts those distant colleagues to the action and in no time that first bird is joined by many others. They dive from varying heights, up to a hundred feet or more, folding their wings just before they splash through the surface like a stone. They do not penetrate deep, indeed their buoyant plumage would make it difficult for them to dive far down, but it is the speed of entry into the water which gives the required impetus for a brief underwater chase. With forward-facing eyes giving binocular vision so that they can judge distances accurately, they capture herrings or mackerel or flying fish in the powerful dagger-shaped bill. They have large webbed feet, not so much for swimming as for skilled underwater manoeuvring in the chase. To absorb the shock of the impact, they have a system of air sacs under the skin, inflated from the lungs to form a spongy protective mattress at the breast. Their external nostrils are much reduced (altogether closed in gannets). They have a secondary nostril system, where a narrow slit at the angle of the beak is sheltered by a horny flap which serves to stop water forcing itself into the mouth on impact.

Although most gannets and boobies have a lot of white in their plumage, they have black tips to the wings, a trait typical of seabirds. The insoluble dark pigment granules of melanin have a strengthening effect giving extra resistance to wear and tear at these vulnerable extremities.

In tropical waters the main food of the abundant boobies is

The Brown Pelican is the only pelican which plunge-dives for its fish. The activity may look clumsy but it is highly effective

squid and flying fish, which are chased both in the sea and over it. Both tropicbirds and terns plunge for their food, too, but from a lesser height, and they hover like kestrels before they commit themselves to the descent. Mostly they pick or scoop small fish from the surface with their straight, sharply pointed bills without getting their feathers, or even their feet, wet. Since they do not submerge or have any impact with the water they have external nostrils. They do not rest on the water, but will perch on a piece of convenient driftwood or the rail of a ship if it suits them, but equally they may stay in flight for months on end without difficulty. The sea terns (known as sea-swallows to sailors because of their long tail streamers) live enviably free lives, many of them breeding in one hemisphere and 'wintering' in another in order to enjoy a life of perpetual summer, always where the feeding is at its seasonal best.

Gannets also plunge-dive, taking swift pelagic fish like herrings just below the surface

Arctic Terns are highly manoeuvrable in hovering and picking fish from the surface, but they are also long-distance travellers

Skimmers belong to a different family but are almost as elegant as the terns, which they superficially resemble. Unlike the sea terns, which range widely over the oceans, the American Black Skimmers are coastal and river birds, living sociably on beaches and sand-bars. They have a most remarkable feeding technique. The lower mandible is markedly longer than the upper; it is a thin and flexible sensitive probe. The bird flies along literally just above the surface, its lower mandible held down and knifing through the top couple of inches of surface water. When it touches prey the bird snaps its head down so that the upper mandible closes on the lower with a snap. The whole operation is highly efficient but somewhat Disney-esque.

Two of the three phalaropes are sea-going birds. The Red and the Red-necked Phalaropes breed in the far northern tundra but spend much of their time at sea. As the only pelagic waders (shorebirds) they are specially adapted, with slightly webbed feet and broad toes. Their legs are oval-shaped in section in order to reduce water resistance yet retain strength. Their breast and belly plumage is extra dense so providing enhanced buoyancy and waterproofing – they float like corks. So they are designed to enjoy

34

a great deal of swimming and indeed they are mostly seen in sociable gatherings on the water. Outside the breeding season they gather in huge numbers to pick small plankton animals from the surface in areas of upwellings. But I am not sure, when at sea, whether they indulge in the spinning activity which makes them such endearing creatures at their freshwater fishing-grounds at breeding time, when they stir up the aquatic larvae by paddling 'on-the-spot' in furious circles. On the ocean they usually fly off long before you get close enough to see what they're up to.

Not all birds catch their own fish. Bird society is no different from our own in that there are thieves and robbers who prefer to benefit from the hard work of others. In zoology there is even a word to describe the activity – kleptoparasitism – in which an animal steals food which has already been captured by another. Those that practise this at sea are of course best described as pirates. The behaviour is most typical of the wide-ranging skuas (jaegers) but is characteristic to a lesser extent of the Antarctic sheathbills, some gulls and the tropical frigatebirds. Kleptoparasitism is very much a seabird speciality. At the breeding-grounds, skuas and gulls will feed on the eggs and young of other birds. Skuas are forceful and acrobatic in harrying other birds, 'persuading' them to empty their crops and then scooping the prize before it hits the sea. Piracy is a step along the road to straight predation, and skuas are a good example of that, taking young puffins and kittiwakes when they get the chance. Frigatebirds, too, take tern and shearwater chicks.

Frigatebirds are masters of soaring flight, with long narrow wings, but are also accomplished acrobats, using their deeply forked tails as control surfaces in chasing boobies or in catching flying fish in flight or just at the surface. They cannot swim or dive; their wettable plumage would quickly become waterlogged if they found themselves in the sea, so they tend to return to land at night to roost. Yet on occasion they spend several days at sea, so it must be assumed that they can sleep on the wing, as swifts do. Not only are they non-swimmers, but they cannot walk either, having negligible legs and feet. They can perch at the nesting-tree, or on a ship's rigging, but have traded an almost total lack of land mobility and swimming capacity in exchange for superb flight capability.

Phalaropes spin on their own axis to create a very local upwelling of food items

35

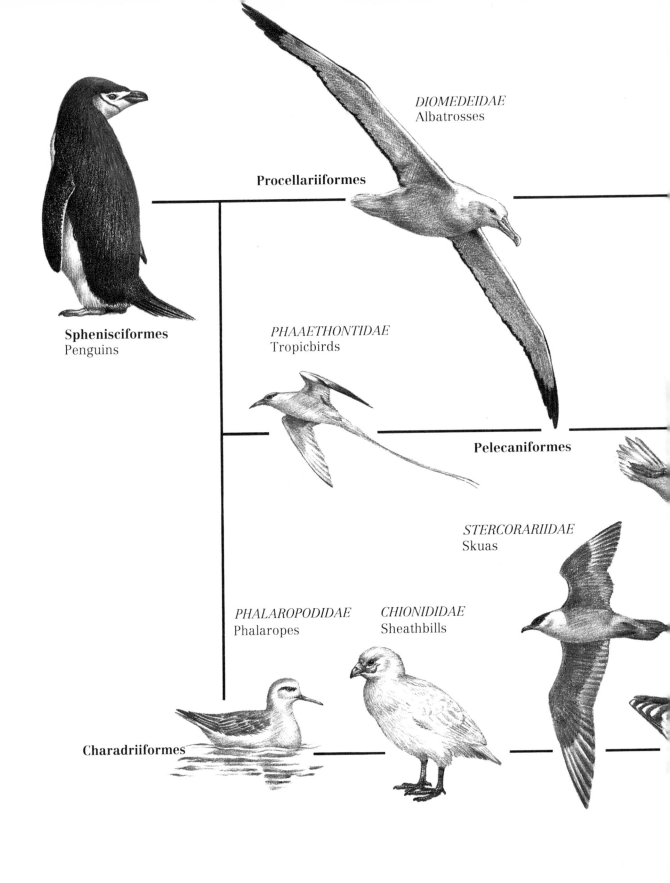

**Sp
hen
isc
iform
es**

Spihenisciformes
Penguins

Procellariiformes

DIOMEDEIDAE
Albatrosses

PHAAETHONTIDAE
Tropicbirds

Pelecaniformes

STERCORARIIDAE
Skuas

PHALAROPODIDAE
Phalaropes

CHIONIDIDAE
Sheathbills

Charadriiformes

PROCELLARIIDAE
Petrels and Shearwaters

OCEANITIDAE
Storm-petrels

PELECANOIDIDAE
Diving-petrels

SULIDAE
Gannets and Boobies

PELECANIDAE
Pelicans

PHALOCROCORACIDAE
Cormorants

FREGATIDAE
Frigatebirds

ALCIDAE
Auks

RYNCHOPIDAE
Skimmers

STERNIDAE
Terns and Noddies

LARIDAE
Gulls

Previous page:
*Representatives of the
major seabird families from*
penguin (top left) *to* auk
(bottom right).
*The seabird family names
are given* (right)

SEABIRD FAMILIES IN SYSTEMATIC ORDER

Sphenisciformes
    SPHENISCIDAE   Penguins

Procellariiformes
    DIOMEDEIDAE   Albatrosses
    PROCELLARIIDAE   Petrels and Shearwaters
    OCEANITIDAE   Storm-petrels
    PELECANOIDIDAE   Diving-petrels

Pelecaniformes
    PHAAETHONTIDAE   Tropicbirds
    PELECANIDAE   Pelicans
    SULIDAE   Gannets and Boobies
    PHALOCROCORACIDAE Cormorants
    FREGATIDAE   Frigatebirds

Charadriiformes
    PHALAROPODIDAE   Phalaropes
    CHIONIDIDAE   Sheathbills
    STERCORARIIDAE   Skuas
    LARIDAE   Gulls
    STERNIDAE   Terns and Noddies
    RYNCHOPIDAE   Skimmers
    ALCIDAE   Auks

Gulls have a sort of general-purpose shape which gives them a high degree of skill in most flying departments. They are fairly manoeuvrable, they have fair endurance and they are at home on land as well, able to follow the plough or plunder the rubbish dump. They operate as opportunists, taking their chances where they may. Fresh fish, dead fish, offal or galley scraps, all is grist to their gizzards. Their wing-shape and flight pattern is a practical compromise between the gliding of albatrosses and the manic whirring of the auks.

Auks have short, narrow wings which must flap hard to make

headway in the air. But underwater they fly superbly, using their wings as paddles in pursuit of sand-eels. They can hold their breath for long periods and they can work at depths of hundreds of feet. In evolutionary terms, they seem so wonderfully efficient at catching fish as pursuit divers that they hardly need to fly. They seem to be on the way to emulating the penguins which have given up flying altogether. Apart from the penguin family only one other seabird has taken this irrevocable step and that is the flightless cormorant of the Galapagos Islands, with its vestigial wings.

Cormorants hunt fish and eels, by free swimming or by swimming along the bottom in shallow water, using their large webbed feet for propulsion and their wings as control surfaces. They are a widespread family, colonising the coast and inshore waters from the Arctic Circle to the Antarctic peninsula by way of the equator. They are superb divers, able to jack-knife from the surface without needing the height and plunge of gannets. To improve their underwater performance their large contour feathers are not waterproof, trapping little air and reducing buoyancy. While their

Seabirds like this fulmar dispose of excess salt in their bloodstreams in a concentrated solution of sodium chloride which flows through their nasal cavities. Since they cannot sneeze they either shake their heads or drip!

dense body plumage keeps their skins dry inside the suit of feathers, they nevertheless face a problem when they have finished fishing. The large flight feathers of wings and tail become sopping wet and before the cormorant can regain full flight capability – important in case it needs to make a quick getaway from danger – it must dry and preen them. So this is why cormorants are so often seen on sand-spits or posts or mooring buoys, their wings spread out into the wind to dry.

Some seabirds fish by day and some by night, exactly as owls take over the night shift ashore and work the same meadows and verges that other birds of prey have quartered during the day. Tropicbirds are most active at dusk, plunge-diving for the squid which rise to the surface at that time. A little later the petrels also look for squid and the nocturnal plankton rise. Shearwaters are mainly nocturnal, roosting by day cradled on the bosom of the sea, when you may come across them in numbers which defy counting.

Some terns may roost on the wing, some will crowd onto floating timber, or ships, as do gannets, boobies and gulls. Coastal species tend to come ashore by day or by night, depending on their feeding preferences, but on the whole we know very little about the resting habits of seabirds.

Seabirds face one major problem which at first sight seems insoluble. There is no reliable source of fresh drinking water at sea. Gulls certainly drink water, the oceanic kittiwakes revel in it during their enforced time ashore in the breeding season, but at sea they must make do without. Inevitably, they ingest more salt than they need. But they are well equipped for dealing with this excess.

Birds generally have rather inefficient kidneys, but this is not a problem for land species. Seabirds have highly developed salt excretion glands in their skulls, which function when the amount of salt taken into the body is more than the kidneys can cope with. These lateral nasal glands perform the function of kidneys, extracting salt from the bloodstream and secreting a concentrated solution of sodium chloride which then flows through ducts in the nasal cavity, to drip or be shaken from the end of the bill (birds cannot sneeze, so they shake their heads from side to side). In the case of divers like boobies, gannets and cormorants, birds which have no external nostrils, the liquid trickles from the internal nostrils in the roof of the mouth.

There is one problem which is not so elegantly solved at sea. While birds can and do go through the rituals of courtship on the watery wastes, they are quite unable to incubate eggs at sea, so they must face all the dangers of the land in order to reproduce. While some – the divers (loons), phalaropes, gulls, terns and sea-ducks – may go inland to freshwater lakes and marshes, most true seabirds nest at the first sight of land, on cliff slopes and ledges and in burrows, often in large aggregations on the principle 'there's safety in numbers'. Because they have invested their faith in developing sea-keeping qualities of flight and endurance, they tend to be at a disadvantage on land. Designed for near-perfection at sea, inevitably the legs which have been reduced as much as possible in the interest of aerodynamics are less than perfect as walking appendages ashore. The long-winged albatrosses stumble about, the frigatebirds avoid the ground completely. With their legs placed well astern in order to act as propellers in water, petrels shuffle about in a laughable attempt to walk. Storm-petrels cannot even support their own weight and must push their bodies over the ground and tumble into their burrows.

So it is clear that seabirds must, above all, look for safe, undisturbed places to breed in peace. And they choose remote islands, unclimbable cliffs, places which foxes and men find difficult to plunder. Fortunately our planet is well supplied with such sanctuaries, even in close proximity to the summer abundance of fish, but they need to be identified and protected from excessive disturbance and exploitation. It is as well to remember the salutory tale of the Great Auk, an abundant but vulnerable species, which was slaughtered for its meat so mercilessly that it was driven to extinction, the last survivor killed on an Icelandic stack in 1884.

As a general rule, researchers have shown that seabirds tend to be faithful in marriage, sticking to a partner and to a chosen nest-site once they have found compatibility. And, unlike songbirds ashore, which are lucky to reach their first birthday, and, if they do, must attempt to raise several broods of several chicks in their short lives in order to maintain the overall numbers, seabirds have a greater chance of living to a ripe old age. So they tend to lay only one egg in their clutch, and even if they manage two, one of them is often lost or only one of the chicks survives to fledge. Many of the eggs and chicks are taken by predators like gulls or skuas, and in some cases foxes or men. Many fall off the cliff and perish.

If they manage to survive the first circuits and bumps of flying lessons the surviving chicks must still learn to face the sea and catch their fish. Mortality in their first year is high: 50 per cent in Adélie Penguins; 75 per cent in Northern Gannets. Bryan Nelson estimated that only 10 per cent of gannets reach maturity and breed, when they may be in their fifth or sixth year. Yet, if they get this far, they may survive for many years and have plenty of breeding seasons in which to achieve success. Exceptionally, Herring Gulls have achieved twenty years, a Caspian Tern made twenty-six, a Royal Albatross forty-six and a wild Laysan Albatross saw its fifty-third birthday. Despite sometimes wild fluctuations in population numbers, provided their habitat is healthy, seabirds flourish.

The fabulous Halcyon is able to charm the wind and waves to provide a glassy calm so that she may float a nest on the sea.
'There came the halcyon, whom the sea obeys, when she her nest upon the water lays.'
WILLIAM SHENSTONE
(1714–63)

(Halcyon Days were the two weeks of calm provided for the incubation period.)

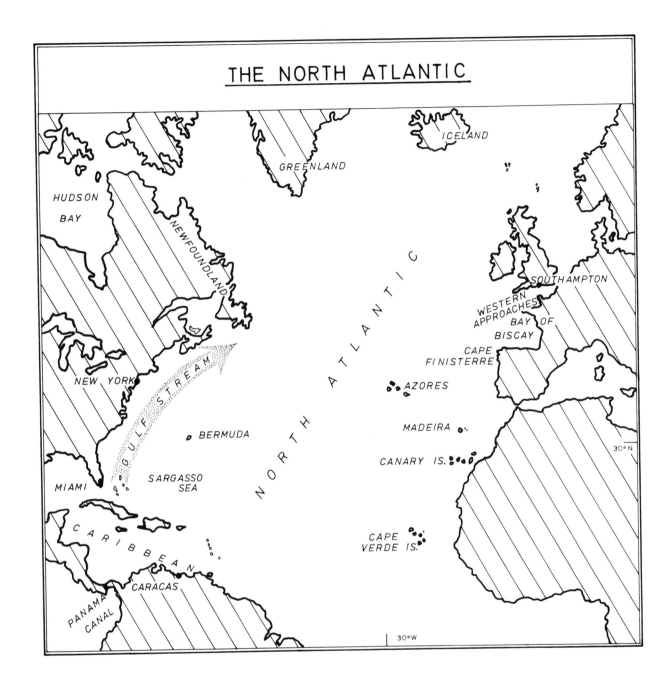

THE NORTH ATLANTIC

ICELAND

GREENLAND

HUDSON
BAY

NEWFOUNDLAND

SOUTHAMPTON

WESTERN
APPROACHES
BAY OF
BISCAY

CAPE
FINISTERRE

NEW YORK

NORTH ATLANTIC

AZORES

BERMUDA

MADEIRA

30°N

CANARY IS.

MIAMI

SARGASSO
SEA

GULF STREAM

CARIBBEAN

CAPE
VERDE IS.

CARACAS

PANAMA
CANAL

30°W

NORTH ATLANTIC

S teaming down-Channel, the Herring Gulls which attend your sailing may well follow the vessel, with Lesser Black-backed Gulls, until land is left behind and you are in the Western Approaches. But they will inevitably fall away, and though a Great Black-backed Gull may persist longer, there will soon come a time when the only gulls in sight are Black-legged Kittiwakes. By the time you have rounded Ushant you should have ticked off Northern Gannets, conspicuous even at a great distance by their whiter-than-white plumage. Curious at first sight that these birds are so white when that brilliance might seem to be a great disadvantage at the breeding-place. But, like most seabirds, gannets breed on remote and inaccessible islands. When they breed on mainland cliffs, you can be sure that the noisy, sociable colonies are just as well protected from disturbance as they are practically impossible to approach. In fact, the white plumage of the gannets serves as a visual signal in keeping contact between far-flung individuals at sea. So when one discovers a fish-shoal at the surface and begins to plunge-dive, others see the action and move in, in turn alerting yet more birds to join the hunt.

Adult Northern Gannets are more or less sedentary by comparison with most seabirds; the male birds, especially, tend to stay near their breeding-cliffs or islands, ready to bag the best nest-sites in spring. But the juveniles travel great distances, starting in their first autumn. The young birds migrate to West Africa without benefit of parental guidance but flying to a pattern programmed into their biological computers. Working to the simplest form of navigation, they follow a set compass course for a given time, making no allowance for leeway. Doubtless many individuals go astray. But enough survive to learn from the experience and develop more sophisticated skills.

After wintering in the fish-rich seas of the eastern Atlantic, they return home to their birthplace, rather late in the breeding season. Here they merely act as spectators, presumably learning the ropes, for they are not mature until they are four or five years old. As the years go by they travel less extensively and become more attached to their colony, working between the nest area and the fishing-grounds. In deep winter the gannets of the Western

Shearwaters

Streaked
Cory's
Pink-footed
Flesh-footed
Great
Wedge-tailed
Buller's
Sooty
Short-tailed
Heinroth's

Christmas
Manx
Fluttering
Hutton's
Newell's
Black-vented
Townsend's
Little
Audubon's

Shearwaters form part of the 'tube-nose' order, which includes the albatrosses and diving-petrels. Their grooved and horny-plated bills are hooked for fish-catching. They are of medium size, 15–25in (38–63cm) long with streamlined bodies and long, thin, pointed wings. Drab birds, most of them are dark above and whitish below, but some are dark all over. Adapted for an ocean-going life, they swim well, having webbed feet placed well back on the body, acting as powerful paddles in water, but serving only to shuffle clumsily on land, when they stumble into their underground burrows.

Their long narrow wings allow for a flight pattern which involves a burst of fast wing-beats followed by a spell of high-speed gliding low over the waves, tipping from side to side first showing the underside then upperparts and seeming to 'shear' the surface. Unlike the albatrosses they do not follow ships routinely, though they may

Approaches will be adults in their snow-white plumage. They cover many miles on fishing expeditions, and may hail from the Welsh strongholds off Pembrokeshire or the southern coast of Ireland or the Channel Islands or the Sept Isles off the coast of Brittany.

Long-distance flights are nothing to seabirds. Take the Manx Shearwaters of the Welsh Islands which commute 700 miles (1,125km) every few days in the breeding season, simply to refuel with sardines in the Bay of Biscay. At any time of year there will be Black-legged Kittiwakes, Northern Fulmars and Manx Shearwaters at sea in this part of the Atlantic, and this is a prime patch for spotting storm-petrels too. Three species commonly follow ships in these waters and their behaviour is a delight to see. Unusual for seabirds, the storm-petrels have extraordinarily long

sometimes keep station for a while.

Manx Shearwaters, which are regrettably not common on the Isle of Man, are great travellers, making remarkable journeys of many thousands of miles between breeding and wintering quarters. 'Soot and white-wash' seabirds, they have a 2ft (60cm) wing-span. In the breeding season they collect in large rafts roosting at sea near cliff-top or mountain-top burrows (on the island of Rhum in the Scottish Hebrides they nest 2,000ft (610m) up the steep mountain slopes). They come ashore under cover of darkness in order to reduce the hazard of predatory gulls, and shuffle into their rabbit-burrow nest tunnels. The single egg is laid several feet from the entrance. They fly several hundred miles to collect sardines with which to feed their chick, which in due course is abandoned to find its own way out of the safety of the burrow and launch itself off the cliff top and fish for itself. They winter in the waters of Brazil and Argentina .

*In the act of diving, the
conspicuous white plumage
of the gannet alerts its
distant neighbours to the
possibility of a shoal*

Michael J Loates.

legs in proportion to their tiny size, and they flutter about, long legs dangling and feet pattering over the waves, for all the world as though they were walking on water. Hence the name 'petrel', 'little Peter'.

The scientific name for the European Storm-Petrel is *Hydrobates pelagicus,* 'oceanic water-walker'. The prefix 'storm' probably comes from the birds' association in the minds of mariners who say their appearance round a ship foretells an imminent blow; or possibly it is a name bestowed by landsmen who only see the species when, as sometimes happens, the birds are blown ashore in great numbers by a storm at sea. Yet another seaman's name is 'Mother Carey's chickens'. Mother Carey may have been something of a sea witch whose 'chickens' attended ships in distress in order to report drownings. Prayer might save a good man but bad lots were transformed by Mother Carey into stormy-petrels, doomed to travel the trackless wastes for ever. Or perhaps Mother Carey was *Mater Cara,* the Mother Beloved or Virgin Mary, whose chickens kept watch over the faithful.

The European Storm-Petrel is the smallest seabird in these north-west Atlantic waters. It habitually follows ships at sea. Unlike Leach's Storm-Petrel, it breeds only on the eastern side of the Atlantic, and is only seen commonly as far out as 30° West. Both of them may be seen in Atlantic waters at any time of the year, while Wilson's Storm-Petrel is a summer phenomenon. Wilson's is the one with the long legs, with yellow webbed feet which extend beyond the square-cut tail in flight, almost a full inch longer than the European Storm-Petrel. Even so it is a tiny bird; yet it travels nearly 7,000 miles (11,250km) between the subantarctic breeding burrows and its North Atlantic summer. Indeed it is typical of the petrel and albatross families which roam the oceans of the world that they start from relatively few nesting areas.

Wilson's Storm-Petrel, nesting in the southernmost South Atlantic, disperses north in April at the end of the southern summer, to work along the coasts of South then North America and then remains in the north-west Atlantic for the summer. In September it crosses to the Western Approaches and then turns south to coast down to Africa towards South America and the home breeding-grounds, arriving there in November at the beginning of the short Antarctic summer. (Even so, it may shuffle through snow to reach

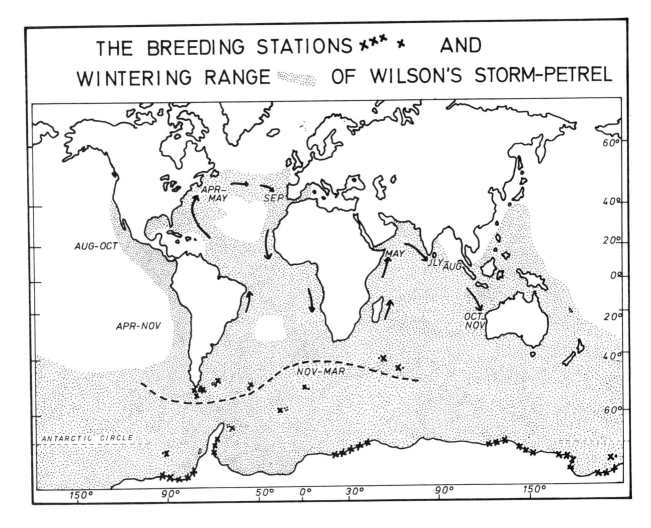

THE BREEDING STATIONS ✱✱✱ ✱ AND
WINTERING RANGE ⟶ OF WILSON'S STORM-PETREL

Wilson's Storm-Petrel
Oceanites oceanicus
*undertakes remarkable
journeys. Of the two
subspecies O.o.exasperatus
breeds south of the dashed
line, at stations marked with
a cross, O.o. oceanicus
(whose wings and tail are
slightly shorter) north of it.
Outside the breeding season
they move steadly north as
transequatorial migrants (as
indicated by the dates and
arrows), ranging the oceans
as shown by the dotted areas*

its burrow.) Thus in its annual cycle it will have looped the whole Atlantic, in a flight pattern carefully correlated to make best use of prevailing winds.

It is in the waters of the Western Approaches that the seabird expert Peter Harrison has developed the technique of 'chumming' in order to entice storm-petrels close to the pelagic birdwatcher. 'Chum' is a noisome mixture of minced fish, fish livers and assorted offal in the form of a stinking liquid mess which was first used by Cornish fishermen to attract small sharks for the 'sport' of shark-fishing. The rather more benign use of chum for birding has produced astonishing results on expeditions into what has become known as 'Wilson's Triangle', an area of upwelling water some hundred miles west of Land's End. The chum is paid out to form a toothsome slick in the wake, and may be boosted with fishy titbits and suet. If all goes well, pelagic gulls and petrels find their way to the delicacies, in the case of petrels by way of their sense of smell. Skuas and fulmars, Great and Sooty Shearwaters have shown up at the feast, as well as the storm-petrels and Sabine's Gulls. In the true tradition of bird-table feeding (and chumming is only another version of artificial feeding), it can only be a matter of time before predators take advantage of chumming sessions, to provide the spectacle of a sea-going Peregrine taking Wilson's Storm-Petrel in front of the binoculars. (There are several records from Falklands waters of Peregrines bringing storm-petrels aboard ships for plucking.)

Many seabirds migrate from summer to summer, breeding in

Storm-petrels haunt the waves, skipping and pattering over the surface and snatching at tiny morsels. Wilson's Storm-Petrel may be the commonest bird in the world. Breeding on subantarctic islands and on the edge of the Antarctic continent, it 'winters' in the North Atlantic summer

No one knows where the Atlantic Puffin spends its winters, but probably most of them are far out at sea in the northern North Atlantic, where they have a flightless moult period before returning to the breeding colonies
COMMANDER M.B. CASEMENT/
RNBWS

one hemisphere and 'wintering' in another, but Leach's Storm-Petrel bucks the trend, breeding on both sides of the Atlantic in high northern latitudes but wintering in the tropics and subtropics. However, unlike Wilson's, it is a possible 'tick' at any time of the year in the North Atlantic. The diagnostic grey line which divides the white rump patch is not in the least easy to see unless the bird is in the hand, but Leach's is longer by an inch or more than the European Storm-Petrel and of course has the forked tail.

Manx Shearwaters and Northern Fulmars should cross your path. Fulmars are everyday possibilities all the way across to Canada and the east coast of the USA. But if, as is most likely with cruise-ship passages, you are heading south, there are other delights to watch for. Crossing the Bay of Biscay and rounding Cape Finisterre, the north-west corner of Spain, you are steaming through a migration staging area for Sabine's Gull, a species which breeds in the circumpolar high Arctic but winters in the far south. If you are lucky enough to see one it is likely to be a solitary bird, unlike the Black-legged Kittiwakes which appear in flocks of varying size. Outside the breeding season the kittiwakes are regularly recorded all the way down the West African coast to the equator. With their graceful and buoyant flight, they take food from the surface, following the ship not so much in the hope of galley waste as for the tiny creatures disturbed and brought to the surface by the passage of the ship and the churning of her screws. Great Skuas (bonxies) are frequent followers, too, searching the wake for titbits. Both bonxies and Pomarine Skuas are confirmed ship-visitors, but whereas the bonxie patrols the North Atlantic the Pomarine Skuas roam the world's oceans.

Approaching Madeira or the Azores, there will be Madeiran Storm-Petrels as well as the storm-petrels of previous days. The Madeiran Storm-Petrels are widespread in the tropical Atlantic. Said to have a 'direct, fast flight', it might be more correct to say they have a distinctive corkscrew motion. But to confuse things they are most often in company with other similar species. As well as Manx Shearwaters, which breed on Madeira, there will be Cory's, which breed there in fair numbers, and Little Shearwaters. Sooty Shearwaters, which breed on subantarctic islands, may come this far north in summertime. To distinguish Cory's from a Great Shearwater, for example, is not easy unless you see the yellow bill and shaded head of the first clearly enough to mark it out from the black cap of the second. The white rump of the Great Shearwater is not too useful a clue as many Cory's have one which is equally conspicuous.

Sea-going birders have tried 'chumming' in these waters, which ought to be good for petrels. As well as the Little Shearwater this area is a fishing-ground for Buller's Petrel, the White-Faced Storm-Petrel and, a Madeiran speciality, the Soft-Plumaged Petrel *Pterodroma mollis*. It may be that the Freira *P.m. madeira* and the Gon-Gon *P.m. feae* are full species, but in any case the Freira is a very rare bird, probably Europe's most endangered, coming from what may be a single colony on high land near Pico Ruivo. Because of the depradations of rats, which take eggs and young in the burrows, the International Council for Bird Preservation has been pursuing an active conservation programme in collaboration with the Madeiran National Park authorities.

Dolphins roam the seas and are often attracted to leap and cavort in the bow- or quarter-wave of a ship or small boat

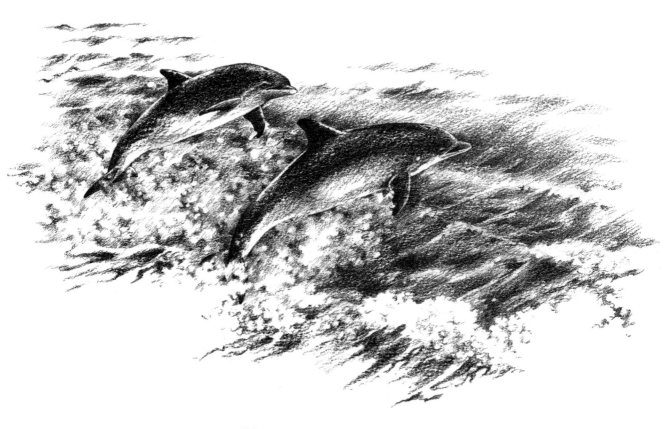

Approaching Funchal harbour your ship will be joined by one of the yellow-legged forms of the Herring Gull which is common and widespread across the whole of the Northern Hemisphere. Check the harbour walls and the town beach for waders. It is also worthwhile to cast a glance at any sport fishing-boat which berths alongside. Once when I was in Funchal, in the month of January, a Hammerhead Shark *Sphyrna zygaena* was unloaded and we were able to have a close look at its extraordinarily extended lobes, with the nostrils set far apart at the end of each leading edge and the little eyes placed just behind them. The sharks are not uncommon here, having migrated inshore to the West African

Fulmars

Northern
Antarctic

The two fulmars are only slightly different physically but they are separated by the warm water belt of the tropics, and inhabit opposite ends of the planet. The Northern Fulmar is a bird of the North Atlantic and Pacific, the Antarctic Fulmar is confined to the southern ocean.

Fulmars are superficially gull-like but stockier and bull necked, sleek yet chunky. The stubby tube-nose bill and dark eye

shows at close range. Their flight is stiff winged, they are masters at gliding but flap readily enough in a calm. Their natural food is plankton and small fish but they have taken enthusiastically to following trawlers and whalers for offal. (In 1847, Thomas Bewick wrote of them as 'extremely greedy and gluttonous, they follow ships fearlessly for filth, they pursue the bloody track of wounded whales, great flocks ravenously pluck off and devour lumps of blubber, till they can hold no more.')

In courtship they hold raucous water-dances near the breeding-cliffs; they are equally noisy at the nest-scrape. Like all petrels they lay a single white egg, it is incubated for nearly two months. After an equally long period of feeding, the chick is abandoned to make its first solo flight unaided. The young birds disperse to live at sea for several years before returning to their birthplace to prospect for a nest-site.

The word fulmar is derived from the Norse, meaning foul gull, from the birds'

coast to winter after the tropical breeding summer.

Heading out into the open Atlantic the gulls, apart from kitti-wakes, are soon left behind, since the majority seldom venture beyond the 100 fathom line of the continental shelf. And in truth, as you head for Florida or the Caribbean, birds are most notable for their absence. There will undoubtedly be Atlantic Puffins but they tend to be widely dispersed and difficult to see. While the other auks, Guillemots and Razorbills, winter close inshore, the puffins spend wintertime in the deep-water Atlantic in ways which are more mysterious than known. But bound for the West Indies you are almost certainly at the extreme southern end of their

Below:
Fulmars displaying at a potential cliff-top nest-site
C.TILDMAN/FLPA

musty smell and habit of spitting stomach oil at intruders. Until the 1870s the only British breeding station was on the remote island of St Kilda, where they were used as a valued resource, the annual harvest numbering some twelve thousand. 'No bird is of such use to the islanders as this: the fulmar supplies them with oil for their lamps, down for their beds, a delicacy for their tables, a balm for their wounds and a medicine for their distempers.' (Thomas Pennant)

From St Kilda fulmars extended their range to other Scottish islands, to Iceland and the Faeroes. By the 1970s almost all suitable cliffs in Britain and Ireland, especially on Atlantic-facing coasts, had been settled. There is still controversy about the reasons for their explosive extension of range, but the increase in trawling and whaling activities certainly provided fuel, though the warming of the north-east Atlantic may also have been a contributory factor.

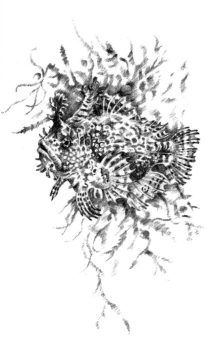

The predatory Frogfish are cunningly camouflaged to look like the Sargassum *weed which they inhabit*

Osprey
Laughing Gull
House Sparrow,
Ring-billed Gull
Herring Gull
Bonaparte's Gull
European Starling
Boat-tailed Grackle
American Crow

*Port Everglades,
Fort Lauderdale.
20 Jan 1988*

distribution. Most will be much further north in the Atlantic, and the North and Norwegian Seas. The population is declining, in spite of our much increased understanding of their needs and man's efforts to protect them.

Though the sea will be innocent of birds for a day or two in the middle part of the passage, there is no shortage of wildlife interest. Butterflies may join the ship for an assisted passage, even if it is going the wrong way. Painted Ladies are common migrants which strive manfully to extend their range, and you may find yourself giving succour to exhausted individuals with sugar-water. Enjoy the long sunny days running down the open ocean with the north-east trade winds. No birds, no ships, no planes, nothing in sight. There will be white tops on heavy waves, yet because the brisk wind is following, the decks enjoy no more than a slight breeze. Perfect weather for starting a tan, or watching for the first flying fish. Watchful eyes on the bridge deck keep a check on the radar and take avoiding action in the face of occasional rain showers.

Look out for dolphins. Apart from the ubiquitous Bottle-nosed Dolphin this is an area where the Long-beaked Spinner has been seen – a dolphin with a long snout, triangular dorsal fin and a deep caudal section. It has the spirited habit of performing acrobatics in which it jumps high out of the water to spin about its own vertical axis. Schools often sport in a vessel's quarter-wave.

In these mid-ocean birdless days the sea is very deep and very blue. The deep blue water is an indication of a sterile region. From the great depths there is no upwelling of mineral-rich silt to fuel the production of marine organisms. Charles Darwin wrote: 'There is more variety of life in and about one leaf of kelp growing about the shore of Tierra del Fuego than in the whole Sargasso Sea.' You might like to imagine the possibility of seeing the Halcyon in these Sargasso waters, since this fabled kingfisher nests on a raft of floating weed on the surface of the sea, able to charm the wind and the waves to produce a glassy calm for the fourteen days of incubation. But, if no Halcyon, you will certainly see masses of the floating *Sargassum* which gives the sea its name.

The Sargasso Sea lies well north of the equator, but in the calm tropical zone contained within the clockwise sweeping of the equatorial current which leaves the West Indies to become the Gulf Stream. This prevailing current both delivers the seaweed and encloses a calm, warm, heavily saline environment. The weedy community is based on a mixture of various intertidal species originating from the West Indies, Central America, and Florida (though it is related to the Japweed *Sargassum muticum* which hails from the Pacific and has been so unfortunately introduced to British shores). Torn away by storms, especially during the hurricane season, some of the floating weed is deposited by the Gulf Stream at the slow-moving edge of the Sargasso, from where it may well take several years to reach the calm central area. Many of the torn fronds actually continue growing during this pelagic adventure and may live for years to propagate naturally, though in any case there is a continual replenishment from the outside world. In turn the floating raft of seaweed supports a community of crustaceans and fish which drift with it. Some species, like the frogfish *Pterophryne tumida* have adapted to thrive in this unlikely environment; they use their pelvic fins to grasp and hold the weed, and their bodies are shaped and coloured to match the branching fronds of weed, to the extent of lines and patterns which mimic the seaweed. Like angler fish, they dangle their lures to entice the small fry of the Sargassum community.

Approaching the West Indies, or the coast of Florida, flying-fish activity increases and there will be some welcome visits from birds. First to show will be Brown Boobies, Sooty Terns, Red-billed and White-tailed Tropicbirds. The upwelling waters east of the West Indies offer rich feeding for offshore tropical birds which breed on remote islands throughout the chain and up through the Bahamas and the Florida Keys. Masked and Red-footed Boobies, as well as Audubon's Shearwaters, work these waters. On the approaches to Miami or Fort Lauderdale watch for Northern Gannets, the same species which saw you off from the English Channel; but now they are birds which breed off the coast of Canada and Iceland and winter down as far as Florida. Unlike the gannets of the eastern Atlantic these have more enthusiasm for wake-fishing and often follow the shrimp-boats which trawl off the Florida coast. Along with the gannets there will be Brown Pelicans, Laughing, Ring-billed, Herring and Great Black-backed Gulls, Royal Terns (possibly Forster's Terns and even Black Skimmers), all taking advantage of the bounty encouraged by the commercial fishing activities.

These bird lists were recorded on actual days ashore. They are included as an indication of the sort of thing any cruising birder might see without much difficulty.

Great Blue Heron
Great Egret
Snowy Egret
Louisiana Heron
Little Blue Heron
Wood Stork
Glossy Ibis
White Ibis
Belted Kingfisher
Northern Mocking Bird
Turkey Vulture
Northern Harrier
Red-shouldered Hawk
Red-tailed Hawk
American Kestrel
Rusty Blackbird
Eastern Phoebe
Rough-winged Swallow
American Coot
Common Gallinule
Double-crested Cormorant
Anhinga
Blue-winged Teal
Cinnamon Teal
Fulvous Whistling Duck
Meadow Lark
Forster's Tern
Wilson's Snipe
Blue-gray Gnatcatcher
Savannah Sparrow
Boat-tailed Grackle
Mottled Duck
Killdeer

Loxahatchee Wildlife Reserve, Florida (West of Delray Beach).
20 Jan 1988, Bernard Watts

CARIBBEAN SEA

Turkey Vulture
Cattle Egret
Snowy Egret
Royal Tern
Brown Pelican
Common Ground Dove
Saffron Finch
Jamaican Mango
Red-billed Streamertail
Black-faced Grassquit
Jamaican Oriole
White-chinned Thrush
Black-throated Blue Warbler
Parula Warbler
White-winged Dove
Loggerhead Kingbird
Jamaican Woodpecker
Bananaquit
Orangequit
Jamaican Tody
Black Swift
Rough-winged Swallow

Montego Bay and Rocklands
Feeding station.
22 Jan 1988

The relatively wide continental shelf off the northern end of South America offers a rich feeding area for wintering seabirds. The Caribbean Sea, which is effectively a part of the tropical North Atlantic, enjoys a surface temperature which may be great for swimming but being poor in nutrients it is not rich in plankton. There are few local nutrient upwellings inside the island chains of the Greater and Lesser Antilles, so with small food potential the central Caribbean offers few seabirds. Fortunately there is a generous upwelling on the ocean side of the islands which provides a natural feeding-ground for offshore tropical seabirds. And because there are so many isolated and inaccessible

Flying fish come in two
main groupings, mono-
planes and biplanes

islands there is a large resident breeding population, augmented by a massive influx of North American birds in autumn. The Caribbean offers an important wintering area for gulls, especially.

Since most vessels work close to the islands on passage in these waters there are plenty of seabird sightings. But be careful, for one of the first 'birds' you see on casting an eye from the ship's rail will most likely be a flying fish. Always flying away from you, a silver and blue flash skims low over the water and eventually rejoins the sea. The abundance of flying fish in these waters is one of the keys to seabird success.

Flying fish are typical of warm tropical and subtropical waters. Although there are many species (the family name is Exocetidae, from which comes the name for the missile 'Exocet' incidentally), they come in two main categories. Ocean-going flying fish generally are monoplanes up to about 8in (20cm) in length. Coastal fish, which are generally larger and faster, are biplanes with four wings

Lisa Salmon bottle-feeds a Red-billed Streamertail at her Rocklands Sanctuary, Montego Bay. As the bird lands on a visitor's finger the two long tail feathers 'whirr' in flight. Jamaica has probably the best birding and the most impressive list of endemics in the Caribbean. Six of the hummingbird genera, and all but three of the seventeen species, are endemic to the West Indies
TONY SOPER

61

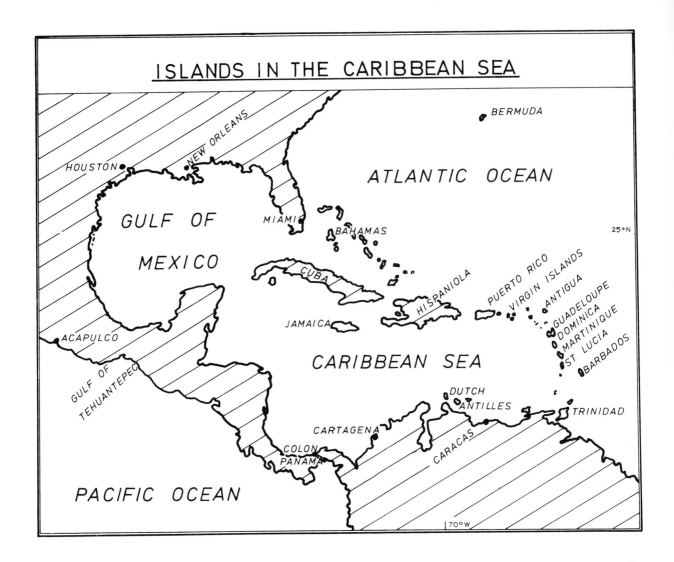

ISLANDS IN THE CARIBBEAN SEA

Brown Pelican
Laughing Gull
Greater Antillean Grackle
Caribbean Parakeet
White-chinned Thrush
Cattle Egret
Puerto Rican Tody
Bananaquit

San Juan, Puerto Rico.
15 April 1989

and reach to 16in (45cm). Their flying has been the subject of much heated argument in the past, when opposing sides were unable to agree whether the fish flew as gliders or by powering their wings. And certainly it is difficult to come to a conclusion from observation, since the wings appear to vibrate on take-off. But high-speed photography has proved conclusively that the fish glide after a tail-powered take-off.

In swimming, the flying fish has its 'wings' folded. But they are galvanised as a reaction to attack, usually from larger fish. They leap out of the water, taxi along the surface and increase speed using a sculling action with the bottom part of the tail fin, which is lengthened to give extra lift on take-off. Once in the air, they will have reached a speed of some 35mph (55kph), when they open their greatly enlarged pectoral and pelvic fins – the wings – to increase lift; the tail comes up and then they glide. By the time they splash down they may have been in the air for the best part of a minute, but ten seconds is the average. Mostly the flight is just above the surface, but when the wind hits them right they have been known to end on a ship's deck or bridge-wing over 30ft (9m) up.

The object of the exercise is, of course, to flee from danger, and that danger is most usually the predatory Dolphin-fish *Coryphaena* but, from the point of view of the flying fish an approaching vessel has to be regarded as a predator and so it takes the instinctive action. In doing this the fish, and sometimes there will be great shoals of them, offer a brilliant spectacle for the watcher but also they offer an opportunity for aerial predators and birds

Brown Pelican
Royal Tern
Brown Booby
Great Blue Heron
Magnificent Frigatebird
Snowy Egret
Lesser Antillean Bullfinch
Pearly-eyed Thrasher
Red-tailed Hawk
Bananaquit
Tropical Mockingbird
Green Heron

St John, US Virgin Islands.
16 Jan 1988,
Bernard Watts

Flight sequence for flying fish – first a leap from the water then taxi and accelerate, sculling with tail fin to 'unstick' and glide

Opposite:
White-tailed Tropicbird.
With their marline-spike
tails and wobbly whistle,
tropicbirds are known to
seamen as bosun birds
ERIC & DAVID HOSKING

Brown Boobies take the
flying fish disturbed by the
passage of a ship
TONY SOPER

are quick to take advantage. Boobies, tropicbirds and frigatebirds will hold station with ships just for the chance to snatch the fish in mid-flight.

Brown Boobies are the most numerous members of the family in Caribbean waters, and they are much in evidence, behaving in much the same way as the Northern Gannets with which they overlap in Florida. Flapping and soaring, they welcome passing ships and, often enough, will perch on a convenient davit or rail to scan the sea for likely prospects. Masked and Red-footed Boobies are rare in these waters, at least in the northern parts, and identification poses real problems, especially at a distance when the various forms of immature plumage confuse the issue. Colour of legs and feet is conclusive. But in real life most Caribbean boobies are Brown Boobies. There may be 17,000 breeding pairs

Masked Booby
Yellow Warbler
Cayenne Tern
Greater Flamingo
American Oystercatcher
Great Egret
Ruddy Turnstone
Magnificent Frigatebird
Brown Pelican
Grey Kingbird Green Heron
Snowy Egret
Semi-palmated Sandpiper
Caribbean Parakeet
Osprey Bananaquit
Tricoloured Heron
Reddish Egret
Great Blue Heron
Great White Heron
Greater Flamingo
Merlin
Black-winged Stilt
Snowy Plover
Sanderling
Western Sandpiper
Least Sandpiper
Whimbrel
Lesser Yellowlegs
Spotted Sandpiper
Royal Tern
Red-necked Pigeon
Eared Dove
Common Ground Dove
White-tipped Dove
Caribbean Parakeet
Groove-billed Ani
Ruby-topaz Hummingbird
Common Emerald
Caribbean Elaenia
Brown-crested Flycatcher
Tropical Mockingbird
Pearly-eyed Thrasher
Yellow Warbler
NorthernWaterthrush
Black-faced Grassquit
Yellow-winged Parrot

Bonaire, Dutch Antilles.
24 Jan 1988

spread along the islands, and they rarely penetrate far to sea, 200 miles (320km) offshore being the probable limit.

Tropicbirds are easy to identify as a family, especially in adult plumage with the extraordinarily long tail feathers. They regularly visit ships, attracted by the flying-fish activity. Circling 100ft (30m) or so in the air, head held down and bill pointing to the water, they wait for a convenient flight of fish; then they half fold the wings and drop in a controlled dive, changing direction as necessary to compensate for any changes of course by the prey, before the catch. In the Caribbean and the open Atlantic Red-billed and White-tailed Tropicbirds are well established. (The Red-tailed is confined to the Pacific and Indian Oceans.) It is the White-tailed which is more numerous around the larger islands of the Greater Antilles chain while the Red-billed is more typical of the southern Lesser Antilles chain. While the juveniles sport no more than a pointed tail, the adults grow long streamers – the marline-spike which gives authority to their seaman's name of bosun bird, although I suppose their penetrating whistle helps as well!

Few enough seabirds make any noise at all at sea, though some of the terns can be noisy at a fish-shoal and boobies may cackle in excitement as they chase flying fish. But the tropicbirds whistle as they pass a ship. It is always worth staying on deck late on tropical nights in the hope of seeing the white shape with the long tail flash by, but more often than not it is the whistle that draws your attention to the bird. They will follow a ship at night to catch the squid which rise up in the darkness and get churned to the surface by the turbulence of the ship's propellors. On the water tropicbirds sit high with great buoyancy, and they cock their tails up in an endearing way. But, having caught a fish or a squid, like boobies they face harassment.from piratical men-o-war.

Frigatebirds are known technically as kleptoparasites; they sometimes prey on other birds, harrying them in aerial dogfights till they disgorge their catch, then swoop to grab it, usually before it hits the water. So to seamen through the ages they have been known as man-o-war birds. With angled wings and deeply forked tails they are masters of air-to-air combat, but very rarely indeed do they settle on the water. Like cormorants, their outer plumage is not very waterproof, so they go to great lengths to avoid getting wet. In aerial scraps they grab the wing or tails of their opponent

Squid are the main prey for tropicbirds. And since squid come to the surface at dusk, that is when tropic-birds fish – sometimes in the lights of a passing ship

with their long hooked beaks, forcing the unfortunate fisher to disgorge his catch. So, when a flying fish has outwitted the Dolphin-fish by leaping clear of the water, it must next avoid the attentions of the predatory birds as it glides in comparative safety above the waves. And when it splashes down into the sea again it must hope that the Dolphin-fish hasn't been following its progress too successfully, something that the bigger fish will certainly have been trying to achieve.

Skuas will be seen in Caribbean waters, and of course they are pirates, too. Arctic and Long-tailed Skuas winter here and may be seen almost daily, but though they will pass close to a ship they do not seek it out. On the other hand, the Pomarine Skua may circle a ship for a while. Any of the skuas may be seen at any time of the year because, of course, there will always be immature or non-breeding birds which are less enthusiastic about the long haul to

Magnificent Frigatebirds sometimes act as pirates, harrying tropicbirds and boobies forcing them to give up their catch

the breeding-grounds of the far north.

In harbour there will almost always be Brown Pelicans and Magnificent Frigatebirds. Laughing Gulls are common at any time, Ring-billed Gulls should be easy to spot, Herring and Bonaparte's Gulls are present.

At sea, on passage between the islands (but not in the central Caribbean Sea, which is decidedly unbirdy) there will certainly be terns – sea-swallows – with their long forked tails and aerial nature. Normally they do not alight on the water but dip food from the surface while hovering or plunge-diving. Royal Terns with their stout red bills, Bridled Terns, Black and Brown Noddies are

Ring-billed Gulls are common around the east and west coasts of USA and Central America. Fiercer-looking than a Mew Gull, they have heavier bills and the distinctive black ring
LEONARD LEE RUE/FLPA

Grey-rumped Swift
Curve-billed Scythebill
Black Vulture
Sulphury Flycatcher
Lesser Yellow-headed Vulture
Savannah Hawk
Cattle Egret   Parakeet sp.
White Collared Swift
Greater Peewee
Orange-bellied Euphonia
Blue-hooded Euphonia
Blood-eared Parakeet
Olivaceous Woodcreeper
Montane Foliage-gleaner
Yellow-hooded Blackbird
Great Egret   Snowy Egret
Wattled Jacana
Common Gallinule

continued opposite

all common. Sooty Terns are commonest of all and should be recorded every day. True ocean-going birds, they are found all round the globe in tropical and subtropical latitudes, breeding and wintering on a basis of 'horizontal' migration. Those breeding in the West Indies fly east to winter off the west coast of Africa. The Caribbean population is in excess of 100,000 pairs, and this is sustained in spite of enthusiastic exploitation by egg-collectors. The 'booby eggs' as they are known confusingly in the markets are believed by the locals to have aphrodisiac qualities. Fishermen have a special relationship with sooties all around the world because these terns serve as useful indicators of schooling fish.

Although terns rarely, if ever, alight on the sea, they are fond of using posts or navigation or mooring buoys as perches to roost on. They will patronise flotsam or drifting tree-trunks, fish-floats and such-like rafts, but perhaps sooties take the prize for the cheekiest attitude to perching as they have been seen standing on a turtle's head.

Tropicbirds

Red-billed
Red-tailed
White-tailed

The three tropicbirds range the high seas as supremely aerial birds with a rather pigeon-like flight, quick, strong wing-beats. They tend to be seen high above the water, and though they are not serious ship-followers, they will pay a short visit to inspect the vessel and greet it with a shrill, trilling whistle.

Sailors have always called them bosun birds, partly because of the extraordinarily long central tail feathers which form a 'marline-spike', but also because of that shrill call which resembles the call of a bosun's whistle.

They are well named, as birds almost exclusively confined to the tropics. Truly pelagic, they will be seen many hundreds of miles from land hunting the trackless wastes where fish are not easy to find. For this reason they tend to be solitary at sea.

They have straight, heavy beaks and short legs, being hardly able to walk ashore.

Common Ground Dove
Great-tailed Grackle
Ringed Kingfisher
Olivaceous Cormorant
Black-crowned Night Heron
Lesser Kiskadee
Buff-necked Ibis
Anhinga   Green Heron
Blue-grey Tanager
Great Kiskadee
Golden Tanager
Black-and-white Warbler

La Guaira to Henri Pittier National Park, Venezuela. 14 Jan 1988

The wedge tails have two central tail feathers which are elongated only in the adults. The mainly white plumage has a pattern of black bars.

Red-billed Tropicbirds range the tropical East Pacific, Caribbean, Atlantic, Red Sea and Indian Oceans. White-tailed Tropicbirds do indeed have a white tail, and a bright yellow or blackish or reddish bill. They are the smallest of the three species and range tropical seas. Red-tailed Tropicbirds have a silky-white plumage tinged rosy, a black crescent over the eye with the black wing bar, and the tail feathers are bright red. They inhabit the tropical Indian and Pacific oceans but *not* the Atlantic.

Tropicbirds plunge-dive heavily, in gannet style, from 50ft (15m) or more, mainly for fish and squids and especially at dusk and night, when squid tend to rise to the surface. After diving they may sit high on the water with their tails cocked up out of the wet. Though they tend to be solitary at sea, tropicbirds can be gregarious in courtship and at the breeding-site. Rocky, remote islands are the chosen habitat for breeding, the single egg is laid without the benefit of a nest on bare rock in a crevice or cave or under a bush. At the nest they are indifferent to man's approach, though they will squawk and peck. The natives of Polynesia have long prized their tail plumes for ornamentation, and while the loss of these feathers may affect their dignity it fortunately does not inconvenience them in performance.

At the southern end of the West Indies, in the bird-rich islands of the Dutch Antilles, there are large colonies of the local form of the Sandwich Tern. These Cayenne Terns have straw- or orange-coloured bills, and the population of 8,000 pairs is confined to the islands of Aruba and Bonaire, here at the northern edge of their range. Egg-collecting is again, unfortunately, a major threat.

Audubon's is probably the commonest shearwater in these waters. Closely related to the Manx Shearwater, it is rather smaller and browner. Characteristically its flight pattern involves half a dozen quick wing beats, then short glides close to the waves. It is widespread as a breeding bird from the Bahamas to Tobago, but again it is much exploited by the locals who dry or salt the nestling squabs for market.

At the end of the day, leave the birds for a moment and keep a sharp eye open at sunset on a calm cloudless evening in the hope of seeing the famous green flash as the giant sun dips. But it must set behind a perfectly clear horizon for success.

Skimmers

Black – American coasts
African – African rivers and coast
Indian – Freshwater, Asia

At first glance skimmers look like largish terns, with long and pointed wings, short forked tails and short red legs. But they enjoy a family of their own by virtue of the extraordinary feeding method, made possible by the character of the bill. The lower mandible is much longer than the upper (uniquely among birds), and is knife-thin and flexible.

The Black Skimmer of the American coast is the most marine of the family, whose three species are geographically isolated in a manner which makes misidentification difficult. Black Skimmers have mostly black upperparts and white rump and underparts, their undertail coverts are white with a black stripe. The bill is vermilion with a blackish tip. In flight they are graceful and buoyant with measured wingbeats. But they spend most of the day loafing sociably on the beach or a conveniently undisturbed sand-bar.

They feed, sociably again, from dusk to dawn, when the water tends to be calm and prey are close to the surface. The unique fishing method is by skimming the surface. The bird picks up speed in flight, then drops

to zero feet and glides or flies just above the surface, wings beating in the dihedral position, above horizontal, with the lower mandible ploughing the surface and trailing a bow-wave. On touching a small fish or shrimp, the head doubles down and the upper mandible snaps shut on the prey. Feeding at night becomes possible because the bird is using touch as its most important sense. However there is also a further adaptation which helps night vision. In the glaring bright light of day the bird protects its eyes by narrowing the pupils to a vertical slit, in cat fashion.

Skimmers breed sociably, as indeed they do everything else, in loose colonies and commonly on barrier islands (in coastal America) or sand-banks. Courtship displays are nocturnal affairs. The nest is a depression, formed by wriggling or kicking the sand. There are usually three or four eggs, which receive special treatment in the great heat of midday. The parents change over incubating duties more frequently, flying to the water and dipping their feet and splashing their breast feathers, returning directly to the nest to wet and cool the eggs. The chicks are well camouflaged and sit tight and invisible on the sand when danger threatens, the parents noisy and bold in their protection. The chicks are born with mandibles of equal length, which makes it possible for them to take food or peck for it in the conventional way, but on fledging they soon start to practise skimming as the lower mandible grows.

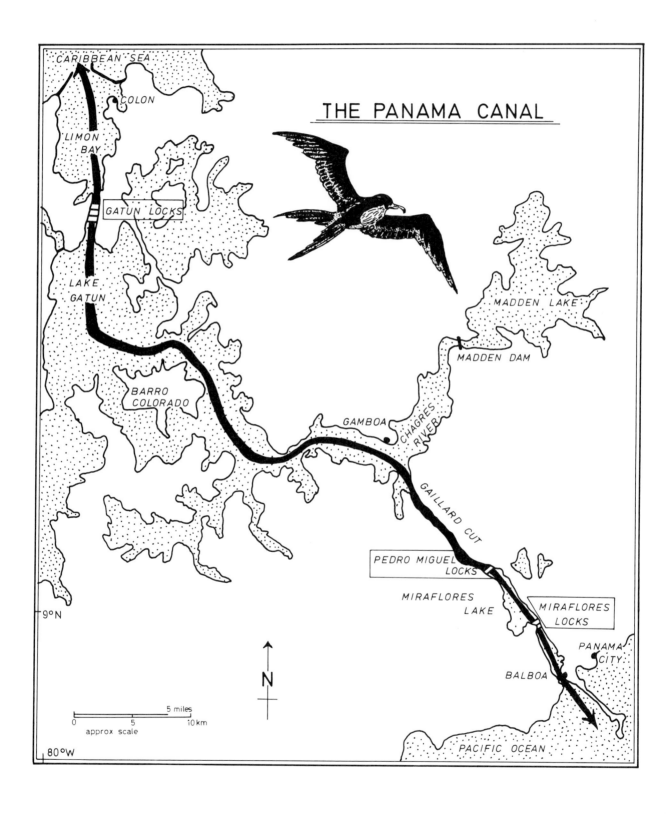

THE PANAMA CANAL

CARIBBEAN SEA

COLON

LIMON BAY

GATUN LOCKS

LAKE GATUN

BARRO COLORADO

MADDEN LAKE

MADDEN DAM

GAMBOA

CHAGRES RIVER

GAILLARD CUT

PEDRO MIGUEL LOCKS

MIRAFLORES LAKE

MIRAFLORES LOCKS

PANAMA CITY

BALBOA

9°N

N

5 miles

0   5   10km

approx scale

80°W

PACIFIC OCEAN

PANAMA CANAL
TO
SAN FRANCISCO

Whether you arrive in early morning or have anchored overnight, you are likely to find yourself in the vast expanse of Cristobal harbour at dawn in company with dozens of other vessels waiting to enter the canal. Fortunately, the Canal Commission tries to arrange for cruise-ships to make the transit in daylight hours, and this offers a day of huge delights. In the harbour itself there will be Bridled Terns roosting on buoys, Royal Terns and Laughing Gulls in attendance as the ship makes her way slowly towards the canal entrance. As the land closes in on either side there may be rows of Sandwich Terns perched on the bankside posts as a first Belted Kingfisher flashes by. As the light begins to improve Great-tailed Grackles come aboard to look for the surprising number of moths which have been attracted by the ship's lights at night. And Rough-winged Swallows swoop overhead in aerial display.

The canal is of course an engineering marvel, one of the twentieth-century wonders of the world, joining the Atlantic to the Pacific across 50 miles (80km) of the isthmus. Electric 'mules' tow ships in and out of the locks, allowing access to the artificial Gatun Lake which, in drowning 164 square miles (425sq km) of tropical forest also created a number of tropical islands rich in wildlife. In fact, in transiting the canal a vessel is raised 85ft (25m) above sea level before descending to the Pacific by way of two more sets of

Tropical Kingbird

locks towards Balboa at the end of the day.

But one of the great joys of the transit day is that it not only provides a staggering insight into man's capabilities as an engineer but it offers a procession of superb birds. The lock areas themselves, with well-tended grassy lawns and manicured trees, are home for hunting Great Kiskadees and yet more grackles, Laughing Gulls and Ground Doves. As you enter the Gatun Lock

Magnificent Frigatebirds soar overhead as you pass through the Panama Canal
TONY SOPER

SS Canberra *at the eastern entrance to the Panama Canal, January 1988. With a beam of 102ft she is close to the maximum of 106 allowed, and there is precious little room to spare as she squeezes into the Gatun Locks*
TONY SOPER

from the Caribbean there will be Magnificent Frigatebirds soaring overhead, cutting the air with their scissor tails as they change course. And as soon as there is enough sun to provide warm air for lift, there will be Black Vultures, in hundreds if you are particularly lucky. There will also be Brown Pelicans.

Once through the locks you enter on the great Gatun Lake. Check the buoys for Olivaceous and Double-crested Cormorants. Soon

Masked Booby
Laughing Gull
Brown Pelican
Olivaceous Cormorant
BlackVulture
Great-tailed Grackle
Vaux's Swift
Tropical Kingbird
Elegant Tern
Snowy Egret
Great Egret
Black Skimmer

Acapulco Bay. 30 Jan 1988

the open waters of the lake give way to jungle islands; these are the summits of hills whose lower slopes are now under water. It is a great delight to cruise between these islands of tropical vegetation, in the knowledge that Howler Monkeys, Coati Mundis and Sloths are hidden behind all that vegetation. Parakeets and Ospreys may cross ahead, Mangrove Swallows flash alongside, Purple Martins string themselves along the ship's stays.

By this time the temperature may be in the mid-nineties, but this suits the soaring birds well enough and you will continue seeing both Black and Turkey Vultures. Ospreys may fish in full view.

Just before the Gaillard Cut there are some swampy bays which offer chances to shorebirds like Snowy Egrets and Green Herons, Lesser Yellowlegs and Semi-palmated Sandpipers. And in the Cut itself, an astonishing feat of explosive blasting which has been channelled through 9 miles (14.5km) of solid rock to provide a 300ft (90m) wide channel, watch for more kiskadees, kingbirds and orioles. Black Vultures roost on the banksides, unmoved by the passage of a 45,000 ton liner a few feet away. They are usually gathered in fair numbers just east of Constructors Hill by the port hand buoy no 1946.

The stately pace imposed by prudent pilotage is one of the birding bonuses here. There is time to scan the banks at leisure.

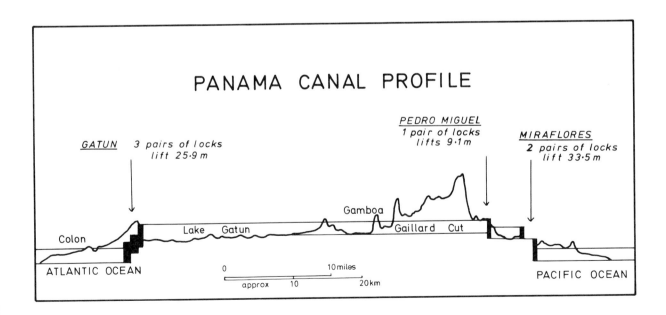

Turkey Vulture (left) *shows a 'two-tone' effect under the wings, whereas the Black Vulture has white patches towards the wing-tips*

Fork-tailed Flycatchers build nests in the lock-side lamp-posts

The last time I went through the Pedro Miguel Locks there was a Fork-tailed Flycatcher busy carrying material to a nest placed high up in the top of a lamp standard, almost, it seemed, within touch of the bridge-wing as we passed.

Between Miraflores Lock and the Port of Balboa, at the end of the day, watch out for a little island on the port side, inside buoy 26A, for a truly impressive roost-site. From all directions birds stream in. Snowy Egrets, Green Herons, frigatebirds, Brown Pelicans, cormorants, Ibis and Black Vultures all crowd in for the relative safety and an undisturbed night. Brown Pelicans are common here, but there is also the slight chance of an American White Pelican at this eastern entrance to the canal.

Many gulls winter here. Apart from the common Mew Gulls, Franklin's, Bonaparte's and Sabine's all migrate from North American breeding-grounds, though the last three are compar-tively rare. If you are lucky enough to pass close to a working shrimp-boat as you enter the Pacific Ocean, you may see ten thousand Laughing Gulls following it, along with thousands of pelicans, hundreds of frigatebirds and boobies. On your first day at sea, there will be boobies with the ship all day (though the plain brown ones are commonest of all).

In these waters you may see your first Great Frigatebird. There will be Red-footed and Blue-footed Boobies, the pale east Pacific race of the Brown Booby, Red-billed Tropicbirds, Little and Royal Terns. The Royal Terns are resident off the Central American coast here, but as you penetrate further north the chance of Elegant Terns becomes greater. You should see them in Acapulco harbour, where you also get the chance to swim off the beach with Brown Pelicans diving all around. Black Skimmers are active here, too, especially at dusk in the bay. Provided the water is calm, they can

Brown Boobies. Right, *showing the clean-cut line between belly and breast;* centre, *juvenile;* left, *the eastern Pacific race* brewsteri, *with pale head and grey bill*

reach fishing speeds of up to 30mph (50kmh), the knife-like lower mandible cutting through the water till it makes contact with a fish, when its head doubles down, the bill clamps shut and the bird lifts away and swallows the catch.

Along this coast there is a fair chance that your ship will be visited by birds which come aboard at night, in error. Confused by the ship's lights, they collide and end up in lifeboats, in odd corners of the deck and in the scuppers. Sooty Shearwaters and Leach's Storm-Petrels are frequent gate-crashers, boobies less so. But one morning, off the coast of Mexico, we found a Brown Booby of the local east Pacific race *brewsteri* sitting uneasily in a fresh breeze in the lee of the anchor winch on *Canberra*'s foredeck. According to one of the hands it had been there since eight o'clock the night before. When we went to look more closely, to see if it was injured, it squawked at us, staggered over the deck and fell out through the scuppers and flew off with great aplomb. More often than not the birds which end up on board ship simply need an hour's rest before they can be launched again.

Black Vultures roost in sociable gatherings on the bankside, literally yards away from passing ships
TONY SOPER

Anna's Hummingbird
American Coot
Red-tailed Hawk
Brewer's Blackbird
Brandt's Cormorant
House Sparrow
European Starling
Mourning Dove

*Universal Studios,
Los Angeles*

Boobies will keep station with a ship for hours, endlessly circling first one side then the other, or they may take a fancy to a convenient perch and hitch a ride for a while. The attraction, of course, is the flying fish disturbed by the passage of the ship through the sea. The boobies are obvious enough, but if you hang over the rail and stare into the surface water you may see another predator which is also interested in the flying fish, and may even leap out of the water after them as they take off.

The Dolphin-fish belongs to the family Coryphaenidae, but is known in these Pacific waters as the Mahi mahi, its Hawaiian name. Yet another name is the Dorado. Almost any name is preferable to Dolphin-fish which has caused endless confusion with the dolphin mammal through the years. Offered 'dolphin' on

Frigatebirds

Ascension –
Tropical South Atlantic

Christmas –
East Indian Ocean

Magnificent –
Tropical western Atlantic and eastern Pacific

Great –
Tropical Indian and Pacific Oceans and south-west Atlantic

Lesser –
South Atlantic and Indian Ocean.

Their name derives from their nature as buccaneers of the sky, just as the handy eighteenth-century frigates were a match for any vessel they might meet at sea. so sailors named them in recognition of their prowess; the alternative 'Man-o-War' bird is simply a variation on the theme. Frigatebirds live up to their reputation with spectacular manoeuvres in aerial pursuit and piracy, stalling and turning with total control in a way which outclasses any competition. Supremely aerial seabirds, they can hang seemingly motionless in the sky for hours, waiting to pounce. The air is their daytime medium, they alight on the water only at their peril, for they have small oil glands and their plumage is not water-proof. If they find themselves in the water by mistake they need to get airborne instantly. They are equally at a disadvantage on dry land, for their legs are short and hopelessly inadequate for walking. They must shuffle and climb to a point

a restaurant menu, sensitive souls react in horror when they think they are about to eat a close relative of the TV star Flipper. The fish is a splendid animal in its own right, and can often be seen to perfection on the shady side of a ship. The upper parts are a brilliant blue, but if they chase and jump you may see a flash of the silver underparts. A prominent dorsal fin extends almost the length of the back, to a deeply forked tail. They seem fast, reaching speeds of nearly 40mph (65kph), but of course they need to be fast to catch up with a flying fish.

Fish have perfectly good teeth with which to crush their prey, but how does the booby deal with the flying fish once it has caught it. Like all other birds, it has no teeth, but instead it has a handful of sand or small pebbles imprisoned in its upper stomach. Strong

from which they can take off.

By night they roost on a tree or bush which offers a convenient launch-pad when the sunrise brings a thermal lift. They have huge wings, up to 7ft (2.1m) in span, a deeply forked tail which is the key to their aerobatics and a piratically hooked bill. With their shapely wings they float effortlessly in dynamic soaring flight, plunging only to retrieve food items from the surface or to snatch a flying fish. Sometimes they chase other seabirds to relieve them of their catch. Patrolling beaches, they watch for an unattended egg or chick or a newly hatched turtle making its way to the sea.

Frigatebirds breed colonially on tropical islands, often in close company with the terns, boobies, cormorants or pelicans whose breeding efforts provide a convenient food source. Uniquely among seabirds, there are striking differences in plumage colour between the sexes, the males being mostly dark while the females have some white on the underparts. In the breeding season there is an even more spectacular difference, for a bare patch of skin on the male's throat inflates to become a scarlet balloon in courtship display, when it also serves as a sound-box for the rattling and yodelling love-calls.

The nest is a bulky structure of twigs in trees or bushes which has to be carefully guarded because frigatebirds are thieves by nature, and will steal building materials as freely as they will take their neighbour's eggs or chicks. The single chick is tended by its parents till long after it has fledged, maybe as much as a year. The young birds are easily recognised by their white heads. They are said to be easily tamed and used by Polynesians as homers, carrying messages between islands. On leaving their parents they disperse widely, but as adults they tend to be sedentary, which accounts for the isolated populations on remote islands.

muscles work the grit and fish together to crush and grind. And since there is no supply of grit at sea, the gizzard has to be re-filled with grinding stones when the bird visits the shore for roosting or breeding.

After a call at Acapulco, the next excitement in sailing north is to skirt the fabulous Mexican peninsula of Baja California. A 700-mile (1,125km) tongue of land enclosing the Sea of Cortez and reaching down from the US border, it spawns many islands and hosts many important breeding-stations for such species as Brown Pelicans and Double-crested Cormorants. Sadly, increasing disturbance by tourists, including many natural history and whale-watching tours, is threatening the stability of populations. It is unfortunate that whale-watchers tend to visit Scammon's Lagoon and San Ignacio Lagoons, the Gray Whale calving areas, in deep

Brown Pelicans plunge-dive for their fish but are perfectly prepared to accept handouts from fishermen or tourists
TONY SOPER

winter, at the start of the bird nesting season. Productive though the islands are, there are few endemics, though the Least Storm-Petrel and Craveri's Murrelet breed here. Cassin's Auklet has its southernmost breeding station on Isla Geronimo, an island that is literally honeycombed with its burrows.

Phalaropes sometimes congregate offshore in these waters in uncountable numbers. Breeding in the far north in midsummer, they disperse over the oceans in early autumn. Light, airy birds, they sit high in the water like corks, with lots of freeboard. With waterfowl plumage, they have a high air-retention and are almost impervious to wetting. Of the three species, Wilson's winters inland but both Red and Red-necked are truly pelagic birds, spending the best part of ten months a year at sea. Many hundreds of thousands winter in Humboldt-current territory off South America. But the Mexican/Californian birds are either at the northernmost end of their breeding range or they are on their way north to breed. Swimming waders, they are plankton feeders, perhaps performing their curious trick of spinning on the surface to induce their prey to corkscrew up to the surface and be picked off. That is not the only curious thing about phalaropes, though. They represent one of the few bird families which indulge in role reversal, where the males incubate and care for the young while the gaudy females make all the running in display and establishing territory, leaving the males to finish the job as soon as they have laid the eggs.

Phalaropes are most difficult to identify in winter plumage, but the likelihood is that most of the winter birds off the Mexican coast are Reds, often large flocks, long lines of them feeding on plankton slicks. They have been seen perching on the backs or dorsal fins of whales, presumably picking off parasites with their needle bills. And one of the great pleasures of the Baja waters is the high likelihood of seeing whales, to say nothing of dolphins, sealions and turtles.

Gray Whales come from the Bering Sea down to the warm waters of the tropical Pacific to calve. In midwinter the cows, weighing up to 30 tons, and up to 50ft (15m) in overall length, home in to the shallow-water lagoons to drop their calves in peace, although it has to be said that nowadays they are usually attended by a gallery of excited whale-watchers the moment they show their

Off Cabo San Lucas at the southern tip of Baja California the officer of the watch saw 'a bird perched on a whale's back' Phalaropes are known to cadge lifts in this way, but possibly they are also looking for parasites

barnacle-encrusted snouts. Slow and ponderous for most of the year, they leap and splash in courtship display. Much persecuted in the past, they have recovered miraculously since the protection laws of 1946. A popular pastime in California nowadays is to gather at headlands to see the Gray Whales and calves migrating northwards along the coast on their journey to the feeding waters of Alaska and the Bering Sea. For they do not feed at all during their

Boobies

Blue-footed –
    Tropical American Pacific

Peruvian –
    Humboldt Current area.

Abbott's –
    North-east Indian Ocean
    (Christmas Island)

Masked –
    Pantropical

Red-footed –
    Pantropical

Brown –
    Pantropical

The name is derived from the Spanish 'Bobo' for a clown with the implication of a certain stupidity, assumed from their clumsiness on land, and their reluctance to appreciate the danger of a man's approach. In the past their colonies have been sadly reduced by constant exploitation for eggs, fat chicks for food supply or simply by clubbing for fishing bait. Their habit of roosting on a convenient ship has provided many a seabird dinner for hungry mariners.

Boobies, like the gannets of the same family, are the size of geese, cigar shaped with long pointed wings, stout conical beaks, long necks and long wedge tails. Their short legs have warm webbed feet which serve to incubate eggs, since boobies and gannets have no brood patch in their plumage.

They are sociable birds, both ashore and at sea. And while the gannets inhabit more temperate regions, boobies are blue-water birds with a tropical and subtropical distribution. Brown, Masked and Red-footed Boobies share the same range, practically girdling the tropical world, the others are more restricted.

Brown Boobies are the commonest in the sense of most often seen in the widest geographical area. But beware the confusing

stay in the nursery waters of the tropics.

Californian Sealions may sometimes be seen miles offshore, lazing on the surface with flippers waving in the air as they lie back and watch a ship steam by. Certainly they will be present in fair numbers in any of the southern Californian ports. Welcoming you to Los Angeles there will be Western and Franklin's Gulls, Black-vented Shearwaters and yet more thousands of phalaropes strung

truth that all immature boobies are more or less brown; the adult Brown Booby is dark brown all over except for a sharply contrasting white belly.

As gannets, boobies feed by plunge-diving and underwater pursuit of pelagic fish. They range far out to sea on fishing trips, covering a vast area of the impoverished tropical seas in search of the elusive flying fish. Unlike the closely related cormorants they have waterproof plumage and can roost on the sea's surface, but they normally roost ashore (or sometimes on a convenient ship). They are confirmed ship-visitors not haunting the wake as storm-petrels or albatrosses but staying 'up-front', criss-crossing the bow-wave to chase flying fish which take flight to escape the presumed danger of the advancing monster only to face a worse one in the air.

The booby plunge-dives are not so spectacularly vertical as those of the gannets, they tend to be more slanted. But they often involve an exciting wave-top chase when, more often than not, the fish finds safety back in the sea again. Like gannets, boobies are 'double-breasted', with a network of air sacs under the skin which cushions the impact of the plunge and also makes them buoyant in the sea.

Fortunately for them, in view of their touching innocence of man, they choose to breed on the remotest islands and inaccessible cliffs. They adopt a wide range of habitats, from open flat ground to cliff slopes, ledges, trees and bushes. Peruvian boobies may nest at a density of two pairs per square yard, forming colonies of a million pairs and contributing vast quantities of organic fertiliser to support the Peruvian economy. Their breeding success is based on food availability and they may nest at any time of the year, or at intervals of more than a year.

Brown boobies, though laying two eggs, rear only one because the first chick to hatch promptly reduces competition for food by killing its sibling soon after it arrives. The Blue-footed and Peruvian species often rear two young, the Peruvian may even rear four in a good season, but the more wide-ranging pantropical species, fishing less productive waters, have difficulty in raising one and take longer to fatten them to dispersal age. As in so many seabirds, the young, when independent, travel great distances, but as adults they remain within a few hundred miles of their breeding-place where they fight jealously to guard their nest patch.

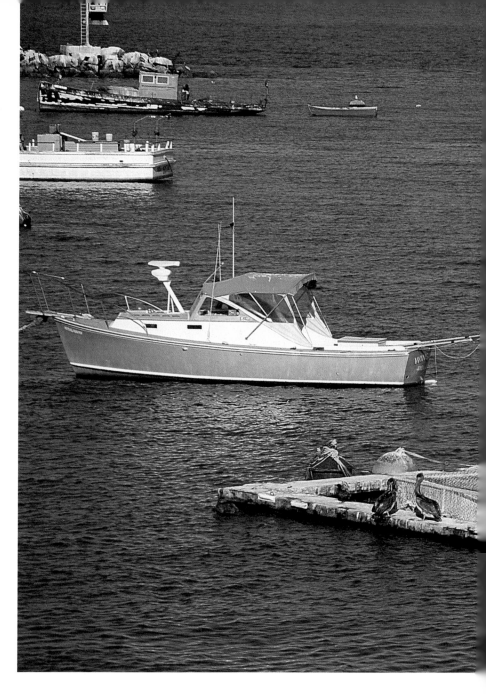

Brown Pelicans roost on a raft in Monterey harbour
TONY SOPER

continued opposite

out in lines on the water. Surf Scoters will also fly by. In LA itself it is surely wise to combine sightseeing with birding. On a trip to Disneyland or Universal Studios, for example, you will see Anna's Hummingbird, as colourful as any of the 'attractions'.

On passage to San Francisco there will be murrelets and auklets, more gulls, including Heerman's and Ring-billed. Crossing Mon-

terey Bay there is the chance of Black and Ashy Storm-Petrels. And even a Blue Whale, for they winter here in February, alongside the Gray Whales. The Blue Whales, too, enjoy the warmth of tropical waters during a lean season when they don't feed, before they move north for the Arctic summer. Once abundant, in all the world's oceans, but heavily over-exploited, it seems likely that they

Bulsa Chica Reserve
Bufflehead
Lesser Scaup
American Coot
Clarke's Grebe
Western Grebe
Pied-billed Grebe
Eared Grebe
Horned Grebe
Surf Scoter
Pintail
Willet
Red-tailed Hawk
Ruddy Duck
Black Skimmer
Black-necked Stilt
American Avocet
Ring-billed Gull
Caspian Tern
Royal Tern
Forster's Tern
Killdeer
Grey Plover
Blue-winged Teal
Ringed Kingfisher
Turkey Vulture
Kestrel
Ruddy Turnstone
Red Knot
Western Sandpiper
Dunlin
Sanderling
Marbled Godwit
Long-billed Dowitcher
Short-billed Dowitcher
Raven
Great Blue Heron
Tree Swallow
Thayer's Gull
American Wigeon
Common Egret
Least Sandpiper
Semi-palmated Sandpiper
Harlequin Duck
Brown Pelican

Los Angeles. 3 Feb 1988.
Bernard Watts

are on the way to recovery in numbers. Monterey Bay is one of the few places where there is a strong chance of seeing them. Monterey itself is a charming town, surrounded by the emerald pines which bear the town's name and also provide good feeding for Red Crossbills, incidentally.

Monterey is worth a visit for what has to be the best aquarium in the world, including a seashore exhibit which is pure magic: Sanderlings, Ruddy Turnstones and American Avocets feeding under your very nose. I can't resist encouraging you to visit Rappa's Restaurant on the very end of Fisherman's Wharf. From the windows you can see Sea Otters (admittedly marked individuals which have strong connections with the aquarium), Western

Pelicans

Eastern White	Australian
Pink-backed	American White
Spot-billed	Brown
Dalmatian	Peruvian

Pelicans have large, heavy bodies, long necks, short legs and broad wings. But their most obvious, and unmistakable, feature is the massive bill. The long and straight upper mandible acts as a lid closing the lower mandible which is an elastic pouch, capable of holding several gallons of water. In order to reduce weight, the pelican's bones contain a remarkable network of air sacs.

Most are birds of inland waters and estuaries, though they may also be found in coastal waters; the Brown and Peruvian are the most truly marine in character.

Pelicans are amongst the largest of all flying birds. While they are ungainly on land, they are well adapted for swimming and flying, with heavy flaps and long glides. They are sociable birds, which tend to spend most of their time in close company. They fly in 'V' formation or in long lines and may sometimes soar at a great height on their broad wings.

Fish is their main food. Most flock in line-abreast or in a semicircle to drive fish into shallow water where they may be scooped into the pouch. However, the Brown Pelican, the smallest of the family (though still with a 6ft 6in (2m)wing-span), plunge-dives downwind with a mighty splash to collect its fish under the surface. The seemingly clumsy impact with the water may serve the useful purpose of temporarily disorientating the prey which is promptly gathered into the bag.

The pelican's pouch is a trapping device, a scoop rather than a dip-net. When the

and Heermann's Gulls, Pigeon Guillemots, Scoters and Brown Pelicans. Californian Sealions will graciously accept gifts of sardines, in competition with the pelicans. The pelican story is one of late-twentieth century success for the conservation movement. Endangered by a whole gamut of environmental threats – pollution, pesticides, etc – their numbers bounced back in response to the banning of DDT. Now the Californian population is numbered in tens of thousands, and the pelicans entertain in every harbour or waterside as a potent symbol of enlightened protection.

Approaching San Francisco you will be passing one of the many exciting reserves of coastal California, the Año Nuevo State Reserve just south of Halfmoon Bay. This offers a quiver of good

Willet
Double-crested Cormorant
Sanderling
Brewer's Blackbird
Surfbird
Black Turnstone
Anna's Hummingbird
White-crowned Sparrow
House Finch Mourning Dove
Long-tailed Duck
Bufflehead

*San Francisco Harbour area.
4–5 Feb 1988, Bernard Watts*

fish are safely inside, the upper mandible closes the lid, the water is drained off and the catch is swallowed whole. As immortalised in the famous rhyme the bill does indeed hold more than its belly can, perhaps two or three times the stomach capacity in gallons, but it certainly cannot hold in its beak enough food for a week, since it will take several pounds of fish in a day.

Pelicans breed sociably, as indeed they do everything else, and annually. The male finds a suitable site, on the ground or in a tree depending on species, then advertises his charms in a ritual swaying, wing-flapping and beak-clapping. The female makes her choice and then joins the ceremony. The chicks are born naked and pink, turning black after a few days. They look remarkably reptilian, as befits their ancient lineage; almost unchanged from the fossil record. Fed by regurgitation, they are said to eat anything up to 150lb (70kg) of part-digested fish before they fledge and face the world.

Opposite:
*Heermann's Gull keeps
close company with the
pelicans and sealion,
thieving when it gets the
chance*
TONY SOPER

*Western Gulls are comon
along the waterfronts of
Pacific North America*
TONY SOPER

coastal birds plus a breeding colony of Northern Elephant Seals. There may be as many as fifteen hundred of these massive beasts hauled out among the sand-dunes. Confined to this area of the North Pacific, this species is currently increasing and prospecting new breeding-sites, but at the moment the Año Nuevo Reserve the easiest way of seeing these superb animals.

San Francisco, as well as being everyone's favourite US city, offers incomparable birding. Año Nuevo is only 60 miles (95km) away, but in less than that distance there are a number of excellent reserves and bird-places. Muir Woods offers Varied Thrush, House Finch, Steller's Jay and the Dark-eyed 'Oregon' Junco as well as the towering Redwood trees. Bolinas Lagoon is excellent for shorebirds, provided you are not within a couple of hours of high water. And in the immediate area of San Francisco there are a number of parks and wildlife refuges (see Appendix 3, p195).

PACIFIC OCEAN

Leaving the berth in San Francisco you may turn through a sea of Surf Scoters which gather here in many hundreds. Under the Golden Gate Bridge, and you enter upon the greatest ocean in the world which takes up more than a third of the Earth's surface, an area greater than that of all our lands combined. A vast expanse of open water, sprinkled with ten thousand small islands. But most of those are on the far side of the Pacific. To reach the Hawaiian archipelago, you face two and a half thousand miles of open sea.

At first the main influence is the Californian Current, which brings cold Arctic water all the way from Japan and supports vast seabird concentrations down the western seaboard of North America. Innumerable cormorants, gulls, auks, shearwaters, storm-petrels and terns. Some of them will blunder into the ship, bemused by the lights at night, and you will find them huddled in nooks and crannies almost anywhere aboard. Sooty Terns are likely candidates, and nine times out of ten the most kindly thing you can do is to pick them up and re-introduce them to the sea, pointing them into the wind as you throw them gently over the side. But if they are bruised, then a good night's rest in a dark box will usually do the trick. Whatever you do, don't put them in the swimming pool, for they can't swim.

On cloudy nights, storm-petrels come to grief in this way and you get the chance to hold these miraculous little bundles in your hand, to marvel that such tiny creatures can live such wild ocean lives. Leach's Storm-Petrels seem particularly prone to shipwreck. We once found one in *Canberra*'s gym, cuddled against the rowing machine. It was perfectly fit and not in the least in need of any exercise, so we photographed it, admiring the thin grey line that divides the white rump, a diagnostic feature which is a good deal easier to see at close quarters than when the bird is wave-hopping. Then we took it to the afterdeck and lifted it gently up into the air and sent it on its way. Some passengers were quite shocked that we should treat such a tiny bird in what they saw as a ruthless fashion; it seemed impossible to them that it could survive. They felt we should have put the bird into one of the ship's outdoor swimming pools!

Worse was to come, for the next day we found that a Cassin's Auklet had indeed found its way into the children's swimming pool and was paddling happily around.(Unlike terns, auks swim very well indeed!) The onlookers were triumphant for here was proof

Surf Scoters in San Francisco Bay

that the birds knew best. In fact the bird was quite unable to take off and gain enough height to get out of the small and high-sided pool. So we retrieved it and had the real pleasure of handling this dumpy little brown bird, and admired the white spot on its lower mandible. Then, to general disapproval, we threw it carefully into the wind. It tumbled and flew off with great aplomb.

Over the days we convinced the 'bird-lovers' that we were acting in the birds' best interests, not working our sadistic wills. Incidentally, there is a lovely story of a freighter finding an Atlantic Puffin in its empty swimming pool off the coast of Wales. Since the puffin was quite unable to get itself out, the crew filled the pool. The bird dived and bathed itself in the jetstream, for it was covered in soot. When the water reached deck level it jumped out and shuffled over the side, none the worse.

Even on the first day out of port it is possible to sight the first albatross, and before many more hours have passed you will certainly see one, for they are common in these latitudes. Masters

An unexpected overnight visitor in the ship's swimming pool – Cassin's Auklet

96

of gliding flight, given a stiff breeze they can sail for hours with no perceptible movement of the wings. Large birds, they have the long narrow wings and short tail made for effortless gliding, and they rarely bother to flap. Of course they are at a big disadvantage in a glassy flat calm, when they are effectively 'grounded', but such conditions are rare. In manoeuvring in company with ships they may flap rather more than is usual in making many alterations of course.

Albatrosses commonly power-glide down the wake to join and keep station with a ship because it offers a cushion of upwardly deflected air which makes for an easy ride. That is to say the bird can lean on the draught. But in most cases the bird simply can't reduce speed and glide slowly enough to match the ship's speed and it must continually describe figures-of-eight or long ellipses to avoid stalling.

From time immemorial sailors have seen albatrosses, fulmars and storm-petrels in a superstitious light, believing that they represent the reincarnations of their drowned comrades, their souls rising from death to become birds condemned eternally to ride the trackless wastes. I was told of an occasion when, at a burial at sea off the Cape of Good Hope, as the canvas-wrapped corpse submerged, an albatross swung under the stern close by the open cargo-doors, and rose up and away down the wake. Such real-life incidents clearly leave a deep impression.

Leach's Storm-Petrel

Apart from the free ride, albatrosses visit ships for the galley waste which is regularly thrown overboard to delight an unseen gathering of fish. (And I once had a fright when a large shark smashed open a plastic bag of waste almost at my feet.) But their main food is squid and deep-water crustaceans. Flying-fish eggs are a delicacy they enjoy, so they alight to examine any clump or line of *Sargassum* weed, where flying fish might have made their nests by drawing the fronds of weed together with threads of elastic mucus. They then anchor the eggs to the nest by the same method, and birds search them out.

Most albatrosses live in the southern oceans, effectively barred from the Northern Hemisphere by the doldrums. Although a few individuals find themselves on the 'wrong side of the door' occasionally, and the Waved Albatross breaks the rules by basing itself on the equatorial Galapagos Islands, there are only three

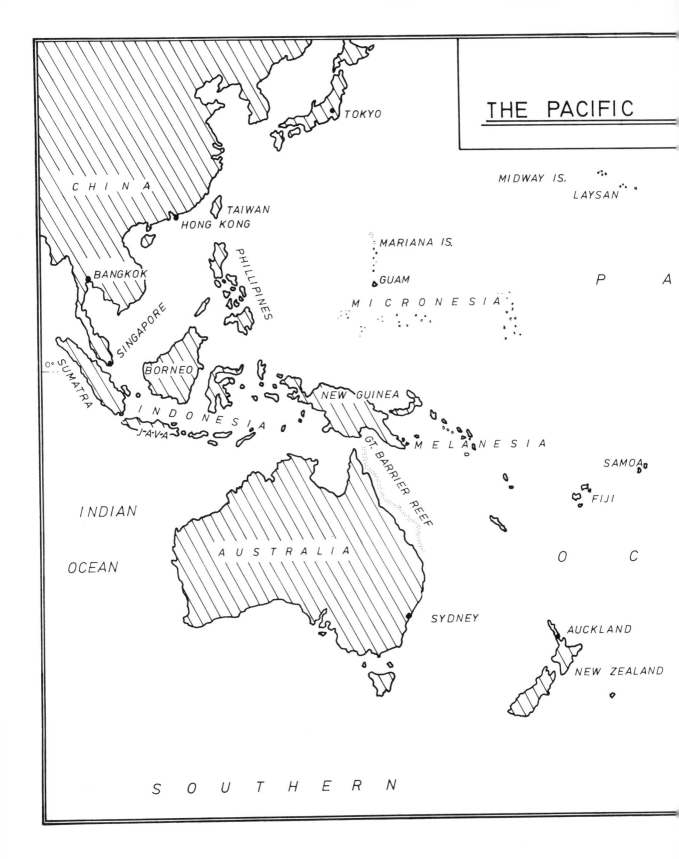

THE PACIFIC

TOKYO

MIDWAY IS.
LAYSAN

CHINA

TAIWAN
HONG KONG

MARIANA IS.

BANGKOK

PHILLIPINES

GUAM

MICRONESIA

P   A

SINGAPORE

SUMATRA

BORNEO

INDONESIA

JAVA

NEW GUINEA

MELANESIA

GT. BARRIER REEF

SAMOA

FIJI

INDIAN

OCEAN

AUSTRALIA

O   C

SYDNEY

AUCKLAND

NEW ZEALAND

SOUTHERN

OCEAN

SAN FRANCISCO

NORTH AMERICA

NEW YORK

MIAMI

HAWAII

CABO
SAN LUCAS

CARIBBEAN

ACAPULCO

SEA

P A C I F I C

CARACAS

L I N E   I S L A N D S

GALAPAGOS IS.

EQUATOR

SOUTH

A M E R I C A

LIMA

CHINCHAS IS.

A N

EASTER ISLAND

SANTIAGO

PUNTO ARENAS

O C E A N

northern species. Of these, the Short-tailed is the world's rarest, reduced to one colony of perhaps two hundred breeding adults on a small volcanic Japanese islet which is their sanctuary. But the Black-footed and Laysan Albatrosses are happily abundant and widespread in the northern Pacific, from the Bering Sea down to about 30° North. Their distributions are similar, and both enjoy the habit of following ships at sea. For much of the time they may lie well back in the wake but, if you are lucky, they will power-glide close to the stern and swing from side to side in gull-fashion.

Laysan Albatrosses have been known to land on deck, when they will have great difficulty in taking off and may appear to be in some discomfort. Usually the discomfort is illusory – most seabirds' legs are made for paddling or perching, walking is something they do badly and as little as possible. Best to get them back in the sea as gently as possible. Face them into the wind and launch them as far off the quarter as possible. But first make sure that they haven't come aboard for a bit of peace and quiet. Boobies, for instance, often choose to roost on ships.

Opposite:
Like all albatrosses, the Laysan Albatross is a master glider
TONY SOPER

Head of Laysan Albatross. The dark eye-shadow helps in reducing glare reflected from the sea

Very occasionally, Laysan Albatrosses may visit for the purpose of courtship. There is a splendid account of a pair which landed on a container ship. After a short period of rest, they faced up to each other and performed the mating dance: bobbing their heads in unison; pointing formally to the sky and then ceremonially placing bills under their wings, only to circle each other with a comical rolling gait, heads bobbing and 'fencing'; all this time making a loud clacking noise by clapping their mandibles together. They remained on board for two hours, providing excellent entertainment for the crew of the MV *Wellington Star*. I have it on the highest authority that the mighty P&O liner *Canberra* was once turned around in the Pacific in order to face a headwind into which an albatross, stranded on board, could fly. The ship was steaming at 20 knots with a 20 knot following wind, so that conditions on deck were calm, making it impossible for the albatross to take off. By turning 180 degrees Captain Gibb created a 40 knot headwind, the bird was released from the bridge-wing, falling at first but then

Sooty Terns frequently collide with ships at night, to be found at dawn tucked away in some corner. Mostly they just need warmth and a rest before release

sailing off with aplomb and not a word of thanks.

It is unlikely that an albatross will ever thank anyone for helping it, for albatrosses seem totally indifferent to man. They are, of course, out of their element ashore or on the deck of a ship. Indeed, many people regard them as stupid birds, because they have only seen them at their breeding-places where they appear superficially clumsy. In Hawaii they are known as Moli's, elsewhere very often Molly's or Mollymawks, possibly from the Dutch mal (foolish) mok (gull). But to the North American servicemen on Pacific islands they became known as gooney birds, yet another version of stupid. Collectively, the word 'Mollymawk' represents the Lesser albatrossses, not the great Wanderings and Royals.

The Hawaian island chain has breeding colonies of both the Black-footed and Laysan Albatrosses. North-west of the group, they have colonised the atolls of Midway and Laysan. In years past the birds, practically helpless when on land, were slaughtered in huge numbers by whalers and islanders for both plumage and flesh, but today they are protected. From just a few pairs in 1900, the Laysan Albatrosses have made a spectacular recovery to something over 60,000 pairs in the early sixties, a response to the shelter provided by introduced vegetation and a more enlightened attitude. Their success has not been without problems. When an airport runway was established in 1935 they faced first disturbance and then Japanese air raids. Because of the serious problems caused by 'birdstrikes' – collisions between aircraft and albatrosses – the US Navy humanely killed 54,000 of the birds, which was no solution to the problem. The answer was to level the sand-dunes by the runway in order to remove the updraughts which attracted the gooney birds in the first place. Now the two families of aviators live together in comparative peace.

The Hawaian islands form the world's most isolated archipelago, with two and a half thousand sea miles separating them from significant land masses in any direction. Heavily forested volcanic islands, they are important breeding areas for more than five million seabirds of twenty-two species, most of which are protected, in law if not in the field. These islands do not offer long lists of potential species for the enthusiastic ticker, but for all that there is a great deal of interest.

The port of Honolulu is on the island of Oahu, not the largest of the group. High-flying tropicbirds and Pomarine Skuas are likely to show themselves on the approaches but the city itself has some real pleasures. Pacific Golden Plovers will be wandering the grassy lawns in front of the public buildings. Zebra and Spotted Doves are everywhere. They are introductions, as are many of the birds which are most easily seen. The ubiquitous House Sparrow and Feral Pigeon are of course urban familiars, but there will be mynas, bulbuls and cardinals as well. Take a No 2 bus to Kapiolani Park to find White Terns nesting in the Ironweed and Banyan trees in downtown Honolulu just alongside Waikiki Beach. Make sure you aren't knocked over by joggers as you gaze up into those translucent white wings. Just outside the city, above Pearl Harbour, is the Keaiwa Heiau State Park, where you may find a mix

Courtship display when a pair of Laysan Albatrosses joined the container vessel Wellington Star, *a most unusual occurrence*
RADIO OFFICER G. SHAW, MV WELLINGTON STAR, BY KIND PERMISSION OF THE EDITOR OF THE MARINE OBSERVER

Immature Black-footed Albatross. This species and the Laysan are the two most likely sightings in the North Pacific. Both are confirmed ship-followers
S.J. HINGSTON, MV SUGAR TRADER/RNBWS

of endemics and introductions. Honeycreepers, Elepaio, Amakihi, Hwame, Laughing Thrush, Shama and Japanese Bush-warbler.

Off the island of Maui, in the Alalakeiki Channel, there is a concentration of Humpback Whales which gather here to breed in the winter, mostly in the period February–March. In their court-ship displays they hurl themselves clear out of the water, flinging their tails in the air in gay abandon. Mating in the warm clear water, they 'sing' the penetrating and soulful songs which have been recorded so successfully by divers. The Maui population, approximately sixty of them, summer in Alaska. Once they were widespread in all the oceans, but there are few left because of their tendency to travel in a leisurely style which made them easy meat for the whaling fleets of the eighteenth and nineteenth centuries. La Haina, on Maui Island, was a whaling port until the 1850s. Today it serves more as a centre for whale-watching, and has a museum devoted to the animals.

Once clear of the islands, seabird-watching will depend upon how closely you are influenced by the shallow water of the Line Islands. Deep water, fewer birds. But tropicbirds may appear, usually flying high, in even the most unproductive parts of tropical

Opposite:
Buller's Albatross. Breeding only on remote islands in New Zealand, Buller's Albatross is a rare sight, but small numbers occur regularly off Tasmania

seas, ever-searching for an upwelling or a wind which may whip up some turbulence. This is a region of equatorial calms; crossing the Line is almost synonymous with poor bird activity (though professional sailors may tell you to watch out for cormorants on the buoys which mark the Line!). No albatrosses glide the wake, for they abhor the doldrums and prefer wind, the more the merrier. Here the sea is truly a desert, winds and currents are circulating around the perimeter, leaving vast expanses of open water without much movement. The lack of turbulence betrays the lack of incoming nutrients to fuel plankton growth. The sea is warm and very salty, clear and deeply blue. The colour and clarity owe their existence to the shortage of suspended sediments and planktonic organisms. Consequently the region is deprived of fish and birds. You may steam all day with hardly a sighting.

The Kiribati Group brings hope, for land causes water masses to meet and tumble, creating the rich mix which encourages life. Squid and flying fish feed boobies, terns, frigatebirds, tropicbirds, shearwaters, petrels, storm-petrels and albatrosses too. Even the

Diving-Petrels

Georgian –
  Subantarctic islands

Common –
  Southern oceans, widespread

Peruvian –
  Western South America

Magellan –
  Cape Horn region

The four species represent one family, part of the order of tube-noses, but they are highly untypical petrels. Instead of flying in search of food they dive for it in the manner of the northern auks, which they so clearly resemble though they are not related. All four are somewhat sedentary residents of the Southern Hemisphere, living between 35^0 and 65^0 South. Almost impossible to tell apart at sea, and to some extent overlapping in distribution, their bill shapes are diagnostic in the hand.

They are stocky birds, 7–10in (18–25cm) in length, black above and white below, short necked and small winged, with short legs housed well aft. The bills are broad based and hook tipped. Their tube nostrils open upwards and are protected from the

water as an adaptation to diving. They buzz about the sky in perpetual motion where most petrels glide and flutter. They fly underwater and in air with equal facility, as 'flying penguins'. All in all, they look remarkably like the Little Auks, of similar, but northern, latitudes, a classic example of convergent evolution, in which animals which are not related grow to look and act like each other as a response to similar environments. One striking difference in behaviour, though, is the way in which diving-petrels treat a wave when flying low over the sea. They simply fly straight through it and out the other side, first in air, then in seawater.

They dive for small fish and crustaceans, krill in the case of the Georgian Diving-Petrel, and have a throat-pouch in which to accumulate food to take back to the nest. They are not normally far from their breeding station, always in cold southern waters. They roost freely at sea, singly or in rafts, and are not ship-followers.

Much as the storm-petrels, they lay a single white egg, though rather a large one, in a burrow or hole. The Peruvian actually burrows into the guano on guanay islands, and has suffered a reduction in numbers because of the commercial guano mining. Ashore, they are nocturnal, in order to avoid predators. They breed early, in their second year, the chicks fledge in seven or eight weeks after a similar incubation period. They were taken in large numbers for food in the past.

chance of a Giant Petrel patrolling the wake for a while. Like the krill of the subpolar regions, the six hundred species of squid offer a basic food source in cornucopian abundance. The seabirds which feed on squid and fish are equally abundant but tend to be widely dispersed in tropical regions at any time of year. Far out at sea they are not too evident unless available food concentrates them into flocks. And, more often then not, a feeding opportunity is initiated by the activities of the predatory tuna. If you see a number of terns or shearwaters going in the same direction then the likelihood is that there is a 'fish-boil' associated with tuna. I have seen a calm sea which suddenly began to flurry with small splashes of white water. The single Brown Noddy which happened to be in attendance was joined, within two minutes, by more than fifty others which rushed in from all quarters. Two

Storm-Petrels

Wilson's	Madeiran
Elliot's	Swinhoe's
Grey-backed	Leach's
White-faced	Markham's
Black-bellied	Tristram's
White-bellied	Black
White-throated	Matsudaira's
European	Ashy
Least	Hornby's
Wedge-rumped	Fork-tailed

Storm-petrels form the family *Oceanitidae* (formerly *Hydrobatidae)*, one of the tube-nose group, and wholeheartedly marine. Of all the flying birds they are the most suc-cessfully adapted to sea-going life. Smallest of all seabirds, they are little larger than swallows, and indeed share some of their dashing and fluttering flight patterns. They tend to be dark above with pale wing coverts, very often with white rumps and forked tails. Their underparts vary, but are often white. They have deeply grooved, hooked bills which are small and black. The nostrils are long and tubular; they have a strong sense of smell, an unusual facility which is not commonly used by birds.

They are web footed, almost helpless on land, shuffling to their nest-burrow aided by their stretched wings. They share characteristics with the penguins, to which they are closely related, though they are airmen as the penguins are submariners. The northern forms tend to be long winged and often fork-tailed whereas the southerners have longer legs and shorter, broader wings.

Immature Masked Booby, tropical Pacific
TONY SOPER

The name petrel may derive from the alleged common usage of 'pitter-patter' from their behaviour in wave walking, the relationship with St Peter may be of later provenance, though it is certainly apposite. The 'storm' certainly comes from their habit of appearing at a ship's wake in times of bad weather, possibly because the ship's passage provides something of a lee, but also of course because plankton is forced to the surface in a ship's wake.

In feeding, they catch small stuff at the surface, picking it off while they flutter. Hovering just at sea level, they walk or pat the waves, picking off plankton. They tend to work alone, or in small, loosely knit flocks. But if food is plentiful they may gather in huge numbers. They will crowd enthusiastically around galley waste, sucking oily drops from the water, or tear fat from a dead whale. Their curiously shaped nostrils give them the ability to smell food at a great distance. Some are enthusiastic ship-followers, though this makes them vulnerable to the attentions of predators like the Peregrine, which has often been seen to bring a 'stormy' to a convenient high point in the rigging where it is plucked and eaten.

Storm-petrels venture ashore only to breed, and they take care to arrive and depart during the hours of darkness, because of the unwelcome attentions of predators like gulls. They breed sociably, in underground crevices and burrows, usually on islands. They tend to be a long time a-growing, breeding at the age of four or five, then a long time a-breeding The single egg is incubated for an extraordinarily long time, nearly two months. Then the chick is fed with stomach-oil from the parents for another two months before it is abandoned to find its own way to sea.

All being well, it may live for twenty years or more.

Large flock Black Noddies
Tuna jumping
White Terns
Great-crested Terns
Pacific Swallow
Common Myna
Snowy Egret
Pacific Reef Heron
Orange-breasted Honey-eater
Jungle Myna
Pacific Golden Plover
Red-vented Bulbul
Black-naped Tern
Spotted Dove
Polynesian Triller
Swamp Harrier
White-collared Kingfisher
Wandering Tattler
Red-footed Booby
White-rumped Swiftlet

Suva, Fiji. 18 Feb 1988

minutes more and the scene was calm again as the fish subsided.

The tern flocks have traditionally served to guide the fishermen of the South Pacific to schools of tuna. They even claim that the behaviour of the birds could indicate the size and depth of the shoal.

Both noddies and terns, especially Sooty Terns, are likely to find their way on board ships during the night, their senses bemused by the lights and their brains fuddled by the impact with a solid surface. If you are lucky enough to find them, check for ringed (banded) individuals, make notes of the ring number, the species, and geographical position, and of course report the finding to the address given. In most cases they only need a couple of hours rest in a warm, dark place, before you release them. Very often the birds are juveniles in their first or second year of seafaring. In the case of the noddies they haven't yet acquired the pale cap, and the terns have rather short swallow tails while they're young.

Most powered vessels travel a great deal too fast for a naturalist's liking, but you might one day see what looks like an oil-slick or grease-patch on a calm sea. This may turn out to be a cluster of *Velella,* the By-the-Wind Sailor, an ocean-going jellyfish which

Ocean-going Terns

Most terns are coastal birds (and some prefer freshwater), but two are deep-water fishers: the Sooty Tern and the Brown Noddy. The Sooty may spend many weeks in flight, never touching down except to snatch a small fish from the surface with a dainty action, not even getting the body plumage wet. They are not particularly waterproof, so must avoid a ducking. They tend to feed in conjunction with tuna shoals, which send small fish flying to the surface.

Sooties do not breed till they are about five or six years old, an unusually long apprenticeship for terns. They breed in colonies of many thousands on tropical islands. Known as 'wideawakes' from their calls, the 'wideawake fairs' on Ascension Island, just south of the equator in the Atlantic, are in full breeding swing independently of the solar seasons and happen at

may reach a couple of inches across. Floating on the surface, the animals are blown at the mercy of any wind by a triangular fin which extends upwards as a sail. They trail polyps and tentacles with which they fish the plankton. (They may be present in astonishing numbers. One ship, the MV *Main Express,* sailed through 'shoals' of *Velella* for five solid days, covering 2,000 nautical miles, surrounded by the jellyfish all the time.)

Not all the animal phenomena will be so tiny, though. On passage through the South Pacific island groups there will be schools of dolphins, including the Pacific Spotted Dolphin, competing with the tuna for squid and surface fish. And there will be Pilot Whales. These are easily identified by a sighting of the massive pot-head, if they are generous enough to come high out of the water and do their slow rolls. The groups may easily consist of several dozen individuals. Remember the golden rule with dolphins and small whales is that you multiply by five the maximum number seen above the surface at any time to get the total number of the school.

Approaching island ports in this area you are likely to be met by flocks of Black Noddies, White and Crested Terns, and as you come

Harbour
White-fronted Tern
Pied Shag
Southern Black-backed Gull
Silver Gull
Black-billed Gull

Auckland. 21 Feb 1988

ten-month intervals. Juvenile losses are so large, though, that the species only just maintains its nevertheless staggering numbers. Other populations of sooties, situated away from the equator, breed conventionally in an annual cycle.

Brown Noddies are seldom seen near land, except in the breeding season. They are striking-looking birds, with a 'negative' tern image, all brown except for a pale grey crown. They were the subject of one of the early homing experiments when Dr J.B. Watson marked some individuals of the Dry Tortugas colonies in the Florida Keys with oil paint. Individual birds taken to Cuba returned home in three days, birds taken to Cape Hatteras on the Virginia coast had further to travel but returned to the nest safely in twelve days.

Noddies build a nest-platform of sticks and seaweed sometimes on the ground but often in a bush. Unlike many terns, which can be fiercely aggressive in defence of their nest territory, they are very tame in their relations with man. They can afford to lay but a single egg as their fledging success rate is high. Unusually for terns, Brown Noddies will often float in the water, where they will plunge to plunder a fish-shoal as gulls do.

Opposite;
Pied Shags are common along the warmer northern coasts of New Zealand. Kelp Gull in the background
TONY SOPER

Miranda
Pied Stilt
South Island Pied Oystercatcher
Welcome Swallow
Black Shag
White-faced Heron
Far East Curlew
Caspian Tern
White-faced Tern
Little Tern
Bar-tailed Godwit
Red Knot
Swamp Harrier
Swamp Hen
Skylark
Goldfinch
Mallard
House Sparrow
European Starling
Australian Coot
Wrybill
Sacred Kingfisher

Auckland. 21 Feb 1988

alongside and berth there will be Pacific Swallows to swoop and dance in welcome. And on nearing the coast of New Zealand you have your first, rather thin, chance of a Little Penguin, and there will be diving-petrels.

New Zealand enjoys perhaps the greatest diversity of seabirds on our planet. Surrounded by deep water but with numberless underwater ridges and plateaux, many islands and outlying reefs, there is an abundance of the sort of upwellings and mixings of cold and warm-water currents which encourage a healthy biomass. Of the relatively unimpressive list of 180 breeding species in the New Zealand avifauna (Panama offers over 500), no less than 70 are seabirds, including 22 endemics. And we must remember that seabirds are usually more remarkable for the large numbers of individuals rather than the number of species. On top of that there are still new forms being discovered to this day, so it is clear that New Zealand is a seabird mecca.

Approaching Auckland Harbour there will be White-fronted Terns, Pied Shags, Kelp and Silver Gulls. In the suburbs you will find any number of familiar introductions, all of them ill-advised. European Starlings, House Sparrows, various finches, Common Blackbirds and Song Thrushes, brought as pest·controllers to these far-off shores by the white settlers who first cut the forest into pasture. But visit some of the wetlands, for instance Miranda on the Firth of Thames south of the city, and you will see great aggregations of shorebirds, including the near-fabulous Wrybill. Catch the tide right, this is vital, and you may practically stand with the feeding army of waders as they work the mud, for the birds here are enjoyably tame.

The coasts of New Zealand are well supplied with terns, shear-waters, petrels and their allies. On one occasion, returning aboard after a day hunting Wrybills, we found a Grey-Faced Petrel practically outside our cabin window as we sailed into the darkness. Given a night's rest in a cardboard box it was away in the morning. A happier fate than befalls many of its fellows, for the Maoris have harvested the fat chicks for the pot since time immemorial, a right duly confirmed in a treaty signed by Queen Victoria. That same historical right allows them to this day to harvest one other species, the Sooty Shearwater, whose chicks are taken for market.

CIRCUM-POLAR MOVEMENTS OF THE WANDERING ALBATROSS AND THE GIANT PETREL

There are prions in these waters but these 'whale-birds' are difficult to separate at sea. They feed in a manner which is reminiscent of the baleen whales. Paddling slow ahead, they draw a current of plankton-filled water into the wide-open gape. A series of overlapping serrations trap the small fry inside when the bill is closed. A throat pouch then expands to blow surplus water out of the sides of the bill, while the food is neatly compressed to a convenient mouthful. Fairy Prions, which are more inclined to pick food daintily while in flight, may be seen in coastal waters in this region when they spread northwards in January from breeding islands south of New Zealand and in the Bass Strait.

Rounding the wild North Cape at the top of New Zealand's North Island you will meet the first Australian Gannets. Like the petrels, these were once taken by the Maoris for food, but nowadays they are protected in law and increasing in numbers. If the ship is fairly close to land there will be Silver Gulls and Buller's Shearwaters. But the main attraction while still in these relatively southern latitudes is the strong possibility of a Wandering Albatross. They are well named in that they circle the Antarctic continent, especially as immatures and in their alternate non-breeding years, but they are mostly found below the Tropic of Capricorn and the passage through the Tasman Sea offers the most likely chance of a sighting in the classic round-the-world itinerary.

The largest of the albatrosses, their wing-span may be nearly 12ft (3.70m) across. Royal Albatrosses, which are also relatively common in the seas around New Zealand, run to little more than 10ft (3m). They are superficially similar to the larger bird, but very much less likely to follow a cruise-ship, though they are said to favour fishing-boats.

Silver and Kelp Gulls will welcome you to magnificent Sydney Harbour, and while ashore you must visit the lovely Botanic Gardens, a short walk from the Circular Quay. Here you will see the exotically coloured Superb Blue Wren cocking its long tail up as it bounces along the grassy verges, snapping for insects. And by the lake there are Straw-necked Ibis, waiting to take bread from your hand.

Australia offers an extraordinary assemblage of wildlife and Sydney is a gateway to a continent ecologically isolated and still unchanged in time. On this mighty desert continent perched

Opposite:
In the southern ocean westerlies predominate. Albatrosses and petrels range the roaring forties exploring food-rich currents which reach up from the Antarctic ice. The birds tend to drift with the wind, revolving round the polar continent. Ringing results from the stations marked by circles show the general pattern of these movements. Main recovery areas are shaded

Waigani settling ponds and Varirata National Park
Masked Plover
Pied Cormorant
Wandering Whistling Duck
Great Egret
Common Sandpiper
Whistling Kite Snowy Egret
Little Black Cormorant
Little Pied Cormorant
Comb-crested Jacana
Black-winged Stilt
Blue-winged Kookaburra
Fantail sp.
Spangled Drongo
Australasian Grebe
Golden Plover Swamp Hen
Common Moorhen
Pacific Swallow
Rainbow Lorikeet
Torresian Crow
Raggiana Bird of Paradise
Hooded Butcherbird
Willie Wagtail
Rainbow Bee-eater
Fawn-breasted Bowerbird
Reef Heron
White-breasted Wood-swallow
Little Corella Glossy Swiftlet

Port Moresby, Papua New Guinea. 29 Feb 1988

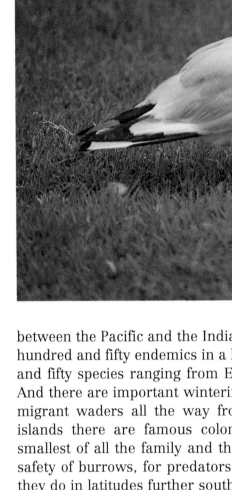

Silver Gulls are common along the coast of Australia and New Zealand. They frequent inland lakes and are the antipodean 'seagull'
TONY SOPER

Red-vented Bulbul
Great Tit
Rose-ringed Parakeet
Crested Bulbul
Chinese Bulbul
Black-faced Laughing
Thrush
Black-throated Laughing
Thrush
White-cheeked Laughing
Thrush
Black-necked Starling
Crested Myna
Common Myna
Magpie Robin
Arctic Warbler
Rufous Turtle Dove
Spotted Turtle Dove
Black Kite
Japanese White-eye
Tree Sparrow
Magpie
Black-headed Gull
Azure-winged Magpie
(escapee)

Botanical Gardens, Hong Kong. 13 March 1988.
Bernard Watts

between the Pacific and the Indian Oceans there are about three hundred and fifty endemics in a bird list of about seven hundred and fifty species ranging from Emus to Laughing Kookaburras. And there are important wintering quarters for trans-equatorial migrant waders all the way from northern Asia. On offshore islands there are famous colonies of the Little Penguin, the smallest of all the family and the only one which breeds in the safety of burrows, for predators pose greater danger here than they do in latitudes further south.

A great number of seabirds move to Australian coastal waters after breeding in the subantarctic. Apart from the Wandering and Royal Albatrosses, Black-browed, Yellow-nosed and White-capped Albatrosses may be seen; Giant Petrels; Fairy Prions; Wedge-tailed, Sooty, Short-tailed and Fluttering Shearwaters; Cape and Great-winged Petrels; Wilson's and White-faced Storm-Petrels and of course the Australian Gannet. With luck you may have a South Polar Skua powering down the wake to glower at you, but it has a decided preference for trawlers, which provide better food prospects.

Short-tailed Shearwaters may cover the sea in a black concentration which heaves and splashes as the birds work a fish-shoal.

Counting them can be a nightmare and you estimate in thousands. Known as 'mutton birds' locally, they have been seen off Tasmania in the Bass Strait in flocks estimated at 150 million birds. At one time they were harvested in millions by early colonists of New South Wales, sold fresh or salted or put in pies, to make a change from the endless sheep meat. Their fat was used as grease in sawmills and coal mines, the oil in pharmaceuticals and more recently in sun-tan lotion. Today they are farmed by Tasmanians under licence, the take carefully regulated in order to conserve the breeding population. In one year half a million may reach the market, without affecting the breeding potential. A truly vigorous species. Like most shearwaters, the mutton birds often come to grief at night on passing vessels, bemused by the lights. And while the birdwatchers on board collect and release them to fly again, dark rumours suggest that many end up in curry below decks!

Sailing inside the Great Barrier Reef provides fair sightings of boobies, shearwaters, terns, tropicbirds, Great and Lesser

Australian Pelicans become very tame where they are hand-fed. Shallow-water birds, they sometimes visit the open sea, and may be seen off the Great Barrier Reef
TONY SOPER

White-breasted Waterhen
Little Grebe
Cotton Pygmy Goose
Common Moorhen
Red-wattled Lapwing
Jack Snipe
Greater Coucal
Green Bee-eater
White-throated Kingfisher
Indian Roller
Yellow-vented Bulbul
Crow-billed Drongo
Black Drongo
Long-tailed Shrike

continued opposite

Frigatebirds. Black Noddies are common, and may take refuge on the ship's rails when they are seen to be 'infested' with what at first looks like a string of fisherman's lead weights. Burdened in this way, the birds are easily taken in the hand after some quiet stalking, and it transpires that their plumage is decorated with the 'sticky burr' seeds of a common coastal tree called *Pisonia*. The noddies use the leaves in nest-building, and the sticky seed heads are used as a cement. Things sometimes get out of hand, and the cement can coat both adults and young birds which are effectively trapped. The birds which we have encountered were still able to fly, but must have been at a severe disadvantage. We picked numbers of the sticky burrs from each bird and released them next day. They took off after a serious preening session, and we wished them luck.

Papua New Guinea, or PNG as the locals choose to shorten it, lies on the edge of two oceans, at the northern limit of the Australasian region; the first thrust of a mountain chain that reaches its peak far away in the Himalayas. It is the land of bower birds and birds of

Skuas

Great	Pomarine
Chilean	Arctic
South Polar	Long-tailed
Antarctic	

The name 'skua' comes from the Icelandic 'skufr' and is presumably a rendering of their chase-calls in flight. Long and dark, skuas look superficially like immature gulls, but they are heavier, more robust and menacing in mien, as befits birds of prey. Theirs is a piratical nature and they have hawk-like beaks to serve it.

Their bills are stout, hooked and plated, with a soft cere-like section at the base of the upper mandible. They have long wings, stout legs and webbed feet. The larger species, the Great Skuas or bonxies, have longish square tails, the rest, smaller and known as jaegers (from the German, hunters) have wedge-shaped tails with two extra-long central feathers. Their flight is gull-like, but faster and with more powerful drive and a curiously stiff gliding effect on the wing-beats.

They range the open oceans but are birds of high latitudes at breeding time. They nest on the ground on the tundra or islands at the extremes of latitude in both

paradise, forty-two glorious species of them, diverse groups which have colonised the island habitats from rain forest to the dry savannah. One of the best birding areas in the western Pacific is the Varirata National Park, not far from Port Moresby, which offers a mixture of dry forest and patches of rain forest in the hills. Here there are doves, catbirds, kingfishers and riflebirds, jewel-babblers and the Magnificent Bird of Paradise. But if you can't get to Varirata try to organise a trip to the Waigani Settling Ponds for Whistling Kites, Masked Lapwings, Comb-crested Jacanas and a host of waders. But you need local protection, for this is an area infested with 'rascals', which sounds jolly enough but turns out to represent fairly serious thieving and pickpocketing.

Japanese ports seem home to an abundance of Black Kites, but there should be Black-tailed and Slaty-backed Gulls, Great and Japanese Cormorants as well. The latter are still trained to fish for their masters, their necks restricted by collars which prevent the birds from swallowing the catch. Japan is also host to the only

Scaly-breasted Munia
Javan Pond Heron
Cinnamon Bittern
Stonechat
Red-throated Pipit
Tree Sparrow
Common Myna
Chinese Goshawk
Brahminy Kite
Zebra Dove
Palm Swift

Bang Phra Reservoir,
Pattaya, Thailand.
19 March 1988

hemispheres, sometimes far from the sea. They are monogamous, pairing for life. The nest-site is often chosen to be conveniently near the food supply provided by a ternery, gullery or penguin rookery. It is not an elaborate affair, just a hollow lined with a bit of greenery. They return to the same nest every year, and maintain a touching relationship with the nearby larder – one pair of skuas to one hundred pairs of penguins, for instance – an arrangement which tends to long-term stability for all the members of the club. Skuas are not sociable in the usual seabird manner, though there may be a fair number breeding in the same area. There are usually two eggs, the chicks are highly dependent until they are fledged, the parents are very aggressive in defence of the nest and young and will unhesitatingly attack a man, ripping his scalp in a power-dive.

As birds of prey, in the breeding season they feed on small mammals such as lemmings, large insects, eggs and chicks of other birds. At sea they force terns, shearwaters, gulls, phalaropes and even gannets to disgorge their catch, often grabbing it before it reaches the water. They will settle on the surface freely for carrion and will follow trawlers or whalers for offal and other ships for galley waste. Great Skuas sometimes even roost on board.

All skuas are long-distance travellers, wintering in the opposite hemisphere from that in which they nested. They may also range far over the polar ice.

Black Noddies will visit ships to rest on a convenient rail
TONY SOPER

Green Bee-eater
Black Naped Oriole
Yellow-vented Bulbul
House Crow
Common Myna
Brahminy Kite
House Swift
Common Kingfisher
Brown-throated Sunbird
Philippine Glossy Starling
Jungle Myna
Spotted Munia
Pink-necked Pigeon
Spotted Turtle Dove
Long-tailed Parakeet
Orange-breasted Pigeon

*Harbour and Botanical
Gardens, Singapore.
21 March 1988,
Bernard Watts*

Opposite:
*The Moto fishing village of
Hanubada, Port Moresby,
Papua New Guinea. A good
place to watch for Lesser
Frigatebirds*
TONY SOPER

colony in the world of our rarest albatross, the Short-tailed. Much persecuted in the past, they are now protected and increasing, but even so only some two hundred breeding adults live on the small volcanic islet of Tori-shima, south of Tokyo. They are said not to be attracted to ships at sea.

The East China Sea can be disappointing but Hong Kong makes up for it. In the breeding season (June, July) visit the spectacular egretry at Yim Tso Ha, where there may be up to a thousand birds in full plumage. And the Mai Po marshes are of international importance, though you must arrange a permit through the Agriculture and Fisheries Department in Kowloon. The reward is the chance of a Chinese Black-headed Gull, dipping like a tern to take mud skippers. This is a bird whose breeding-place is still unknown. Swinhoe's Egret and the Spoon-billed Sandpiper will be there, though these too are rare.

Like its eastern cousin, the South China Sea can be fairly birdless, apart from the odd Streaked Shearwater, Buller's Petrel and perhaps a Masked Booby. Streaked Shearwaters may create a diversion as they bank to and fro in easy flight, keeping station on the beam. The wing streaking shows clearly enough if they bank across the sunlight. Your trip might be enlivened, as one of ours was, when the elegant Crow-billed Drongo hitched a lift and dangled its lyre-shaped tail from a perch in the rigging.

Thailand is famous for wintering palearctic species and its tropical avifauna. From the port of Pattaya it is but a short drive to the Bang Phra Reservoir where even a couple of hours will pay dividends.

The passage to Singapore is likely to be unrewarding, and even the harbour can be a disappointment, with House Crows and the ubiquitous Black Kites leavened by Barn Swallows. The odd Osprey may be seen along Clifford Pier, hunting by the high-rise office blocks! But the Botanical Gardens are good value.

Port Kelang, the port for Kuala Lumpur, may prove rewarding. The fields and ditches by the road behind the container berth should show Wood, Common and Marsh Sandpipers, Brahminy Kite and Little Heron. Collared Kingfishers plunge into the tidal mud at low water for Fiddler Crabs.

Roseate Terns may follow the ship as she sails, and around the corner is the Indian Ocean.

Crow-billed Drongo

Brahminy Kite
Shikra
Tawny Eagle
Spotted Dove
Ring-necked Parakeet
Pied Crested Cuckoo
Coucal
Spotted Owlet
Palm Swift
Bee-eater sp.
Coppersmith
Crimson-breasted Barbet
Lesser Golden-backed
Woodpecker
Red-rumped Swallow
Black Drongo
Common Myna
Jungle Crow
House Crow
Common Iora
Red-whiskered Bulbul
White-browed Bulbul
Black Bulbul
Large Grey Babbler
White-headed Babbler
Brown Flycatcher
Lesser Whitethroat
Booted Warbler
Olivaceous Leaf Warbler
Tailor Bird
Forest Wagtail
Purple-rumped Sunbird
House Sparrow
Stone Curlew

Guindy National Park,
southern suburbs of
Madras. 1 April 1987.
Bob Watts

INDIAN OCEAN

The tropical Indian Ocean is a great place for a sun-tan but of all the seas it is the least rich in birds. Seasonal monsoons give way to long periods of calm, and the high temperature of the surface water makes it barren except where a few cold-water upwellings allow for life. Low food production equals few birds.

The Bay of Bengal will show a few flying fish and perhaps the odd Pomarine Skua. Nearing the Indian sub-continent a whale may blow and a school of dolphins leap and dance in the wake. Approaching the harbour of Madras, the fleet of lugsail rafts which fishes inshore will be accompanied by Crested Terns and there will be Indian Black-headed Gulls around the berth. In inshore waters Crested Terns follow the ship and if there is a brackish lagoon nearby marsh terns like the Whiskered may show.

Colombo harbour may be more productive, both Lesser Crested and Crested Terns joined by Gull-billed, and in the vicinity there will be Brahminy Kite, White-breasted Kingfisher and various drongos.

Unless you sail very close to the Maldive or Laccadive Islands you will miss the Black-naped Tern, but there is always the chance of a Humpback Whale blowing, or a Manta Ray lazing along the surface. Although they are reluctant to show themselves, these islands are home for hundreds of thousands, possibly millions of Brown and Lesser Noddies and Wedge-tailed Shearwaters. Bird

Island in the Seychelles is said to have been home for a possible three million breeding Sooty Terns in the nineteenth century. Nowadays the figure is less than half a million – man's influence has been profound in these islands. Quite apart from the disastrous introduction of exotic animals like goats, rats and rabbits, he harvested eggs and chicks on a grand scale and, perhaps most seriously of all, he altered the vegetation of the islands. Guano-harvesting, for example, literally removes the soil, leaving no bushes for boobies to nest in. And clearing the natural scrub to make way for coconut plantations has effectively barred much of the land to seabirds.

As mutton birds were harvested in Australia and New Zealand, so Wedge-tailed Shearwaters have been taken in enormous numbers here in the tropical Indian Ocean. Until the island was declared a reserve in 1968, ten thousand chicks were taken for salting and sale in local markets from Cousin Island. Sooty Tern

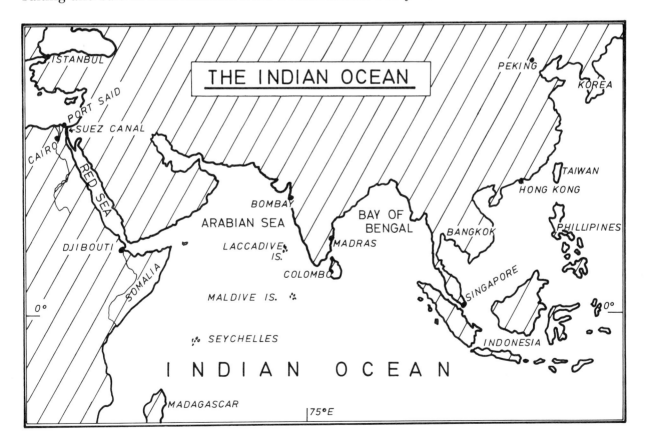

eggs are still taken in the Seychelles, but instead of the suspected five million a year in the old days the current annual take is less than a million.

Bird protection is well advanced in the Seychelles, where the Roseate Terns are cared for on the island of Aride, for instance, making it an important breeding-station since the species is much persecuted elsewhere. But the White-tailed Tropicbird, which was once widespread in the islands, has now retreated to just a few high altitude moss forests.

In the summertime there will be Wilson's Storm-Petrels off the coasts of Africa and the west coast of India, birds which have migrated north from their subantarctic and Antarctic breeding-places. In the month of September they are common and widespread in flocks of up to a hundred individuals. They concentrate around the offshore oil-rigs 70 miles (115km) from Bombay in the Bombay High Oilfield. Each manned platform has an attendant flock milling about downstream waiting for handouts from the galley.

Reaching across to the African side of the Arabian Sea, and as you begin to approach the coast of Somalia, there may be White-bellied Storm-Petrels and more Red-billed Tropicbirds. There are fierce coastal currents here, reaching as much as 7 knots; they lift abyssal water upwards to create more favourable conditions for plankton production and, in turn, fish. So birds are back again. Sooty Gulls will begin to appear. They are confined to this region, their range overlapping with the slightly smaller White-eyed Gull which is more typical of the Red Sea. Both are quite unlike any other gull, with their brown or jet-black hoods and dark plumage and white dashes above and below the eyes.

Brown Boobies and a few Masked Boobies breed on islands at the southern end of the Red Sea. And there is a slightly larger and longer-billed form of Audubon's Shearwater found here, sometimes known as the Persian Shearwater.

Djibouti is not top of the list of most mariners' favourite ports. They call here to water ship, not because they regard it as a social hot-spot. But do not miss the chance of a visit if you are looking for birds. From the Pink-backed Pelicans and Goliath Herons of the harbour to the Abdim Storks, Sacred Ibis and Steppe Eagles of the local rubbish dump, it is a world-class ornithological visit. You will

Goldfronted Chloropsis
Magpie Robin
Palm Swift
Common Sandpiper
Little Egret
Common Myna
White-rumped Swift
Tailorbird
Indian Black-headed Gull
Whiskered Tern
Crested Tern
Intermediate Egret
Jungle Crow
Brahminy Kite
Black Kite
Ring-necked Parakeet
White-breasted Kingfisher
Great Cormorant
Indian Shag
Little Cormorant
Gull-billed Tern

Colombo, Sri Lanka.
28 March 1988,
Bernard Watts

probably see your first White-eyed Gulls around the dock, and there are flamingoes along the brackish pools behind the nearby beach. But scan the list we made (see p126–7) in just four hours one April afternoon to get something of the flavour of the place. And that included time taken for a superb lunch by the beach at Doralé; we ate alongside a small sea-puddle where single specimens of various waders paraded in front of us one by one, totally indifferent to the noisy party of oilmen downing pints just yards away.

The Red Sea presumably gets its name from the occasional blooms of plankton which blossom into what is sometimes known as a 'red tide'. A microscopic plant called *Trichodesmium* congregates in reddish-brown bundles on the surface, appearing like miles of sawdust streaks. Or again, countless millions of a tiny Dinoflagellate called *Noctiluca* can cover the sea with what looks like red sand (not to be confused with the genuine red sand which may be blowing on the wind and getting in your eyes and up your nose!). *Noctiluca* is an animal the size of a pinhead with an orange-red centre, but it may be present in such astronomical numbers that it changes the colour of the sea. Blown ashore in hundreds of tons, it can pile up to create what appears to be a beach of blood.

Barred Ground Dove
Seychelles Blue Pigeon
Great Frigatebird
Indian Myna
Cattle Egret
Seychelles Sunbird
White-tailed Tropicbird
White Tern
Wedge-tailed Shearwater
Common Noddy
Roseate Tern

Mahé, Seychelles.
25 Feb 1986

At night, *Noctiluca* can cause the sea to glow, especially when it is disturbed by the passage of a ship. But it is not the only animal which produces flashes of illumination in the seas. Many fish use lights both to attract and to discover prey. And general phosphorescence may be caused by marine bacteria. Dinoflagellates are the commonest source, and late summer is the most productive time to see the fireworks.

The ship's lights themselves attract not only birds but also insects to come aboard. And especially in these Afro-Arab waters they may swarm in large numbers. One of the barmen on *Canberra* told of a voyage in which locusts came aboard in such quantities that they blocked the vents and sent the public-room temperatures soaring. And landbirds are enthusiastic visitors to a ship at her berth to sample the moths, bees, bugs and insects of all kinds. Very often, they sail with the ship as stowaways.

When *Canberra* sailed from Djibouti not long before dusk, bound by way of the Red Sea for Suez, Sooty Gulls followed in the wake, but two Yellow Wagtails kept closer company, swooping and 'chissicking' about as they chased insects in the deck lights. As the daylight began to fade, they found their way to the exclusive Captain's deck, just behind and below the bridge. On this relatively sheltered sanctuary there were three small bushes in tubs, relics of a grand party in Sydney, and quite the only things reminiscent of a shrubbery or copse on the whole above-decks part of the ship. These long-suffering plants had travelled a good few thousand miles through several seas yet they were in good heart and invitingly green and shrubby. We suddenly realised that one of the wagtails was walking up and down the rail, considering the virtues of these bushes as a roosting-place. As we watched from a discreet distance the bird bounced jauntily into the Weeping Fig , only to be promptly disturbed by a passing seaman who happened to brush past the bush. The bird simply flew across to the other Weeping Fig and settled for the night. Next day it was gone, but droppings decorated the teak deck. Later, in the Mediterranean, these bushes survived to play host to an astonishing procession of guests.

White-eyed Gulls are a Red Sea speciality, becoming less common the farther north you go, still plentiful at the Suez anchorage but not so evident in Port Said harbour. Great Black-headed Gulls may be plentiful at Suez, if you're lucky. The Suez Canal will be good value, especially if you sail late enough in the morning to allow the sun to warm up the thermals for birds of prey. In mid-April the Honey Buzzards will be starting to funnel through on their way to the forests of Central Europe. By the beginning of May the migrants will be crossing the Mediterranean in hundreds of thousands in a single day. Many of them will fly over Suez. Long-legged Buzzards may be counted in tens, Steppe Buzzards in hundreds, Spotted Eagles as single birds.

On both banks the desert creeps up to the canal, and where there is cultivation or engineering works and a shallow lagoon there will be Spur-winged Plovers and perhaps a Greater Flamingo. Pied Kingfishers flash by, Lesser Black-backed and Slender-billed Gulls patrol the waterway.

From Cairo there are annual bird-cruises sponsored by the Royal Society for the Protection of Birds and carried out in style by Swan Hellenic. Tim Stowe was leader of an autumn cruise in the MS *Nile Star* in 1987; he saw a lot of birds, starting in the city. . .

Thursday 24 September

Those up at dawn were rewarded with the sight of hundreds of Cattle Egrets leaving their roost in the zoo gardens and heading out over the city to feed. A single Black Kite joined them for a while. In the zoo grounds, Palm Doves, Hoopoes and Hooded Crows were to be found. Watching from the *Nile Star* provided our first views of the Egyptian race of swallow, as well as migrant swallows from further north.

The trip to the Fayoum started well with close views of a Hoopoe Lark beside the road. At Lake Qarun a bewildering assortment of waders fed on the shores. Hundreds of Little Stints, Little Ringed, Ringed and Kentish Plovers, Redshanks and Greenshanks were watched, sometimes at close range. Over 100 Slender-billed Gulls were also present on the lake, with egrets and terns. A Great Grey Shrike and a Graceful Warbler were seen, and an elusive Osprey circled high above the road.

A short visit to some flooded fields several kilometres from the lake produced several Spur-winged Plovers, Wood Sandpipers and Ruffs, and close views of Black-shouldered Kites sitting on the telegraph poles.

Pygmy Sunbird
Shining Sunbird
Grey Plover
Redshank
Sanderling
Terek Sandpiper
Common Sandpiper
Curlew
Lesser Sand Plover
Oystercatcher
Ringed Plover
Ruddy Turnstone
Reef Heron (dark phase)
Striated Heron
Greenshank
Great White Egret
Little Egret
Black-crowned Finch Lark
Desert Warbler
Great Grey Shrike
Palm Dove
Namaqua Dove
Turtle Dove
Arabian Golden Sparrow
Waxbill sp.
Common Bulbul
Red-backed Shrike

Djibouti. 2 April 1988

The rubbish dump of Djibouti is a prime scavenging area for Abdim's Storks and Sacred Ibis
TONY SOPER

Friday 25 September

At dawn, six Black Kites and large numbers of Cattle Egrets were seen over the zoo gardens from the *Nile Star*. At Sakkara, we saw our first Little Green Bee-eaters as we drove to the Pyramid of Zoser, and several more were seen and heard overhead while we visited the site.

Cruising on the Nile in the afternoon gave us a taste of the wealth of birdlife to be seen from the *Nile Star*, including Spoonbills, Squacco Herons, Purple Gallinules, Marsh Harriers, Black-shouldered Kites, Stone Curlews, Senegal Thick-knees and over 100 Collared Pratincoles. In the evening we docked at El Wasta, where late into the evening Senegal Thick-knees flew over the boat calling.

Several Hoopoes and Crested Larks were seen on the banks, as well as parties of Yellow Wagtails of several races including the black-headed Egyptian race.

Saturday 26 September

At dawn a Spoonbill was seen in the mist, and our first bulbul showed briefly in trees near the boat. The visit to the pyramid at Meydum produced many Kestrels and an unidentified harrier. The walk through the fields afterwards was more productive. Red Avadavats were seen and a Senegal Coucal flew across our path. Many European Bee-eaters were feeding over the fields, where Graceful Warblers and Fan-tailed Warblers were also recorded.

Cruising on the Nile was particularly good. Large numbers of Spur-winged Plovers were seen. New birds for the trip so far included Little Grebe, Teal, Mallard, Garganey, Black-tailed Godwit, Isabelline and Common Wheatears, Clamourous Reed Warbler and a Brown-necked Raven over some distant crags.

Sunday 27 September

As we cruised further up the Nile, herons and egrets became more common. Cattle Egrets probably numbered over 1,000 today. Purple Herons, Pied Kingfishers and Swifts were seen for the first time and Black-shouldered Kites were especially numerous. Dunlin were positively identified for the first time – several probables having been recorded since the first day. All three bee-eaters were seen. At Beni Hassan, Rock Martins were recorded, and in the late

Lesser Black-backed Gull
Garganey
Pomarine Skua
White-eyed Gull
Common Tern
Indian House Crow
Little Tern
Grey Heron
Common Bulbul
Turtle Dove
Spur-winged Plover
Spotted Eagles, 7
Steppe Buzzard, 100s
Egyptian Vulture
Teal
Pintail
Spotted Redshank
Little Tern
Greater Flamingo
Slender-billed Gull
Hoopoe
Bee-eater sp.
Sand Martin
Lesser Pied Kingfisher
Curlew
Hooded Crow
Brown-necked Raven
Barn Swallow
Common Swift
House Martin
Cattle Egret
Merlin
Crested Lark
Black-winged Stilt
Black Kite
Grey Plover
Herring Gull

Suez Canal, Suez–Port Said.
6 April 1988

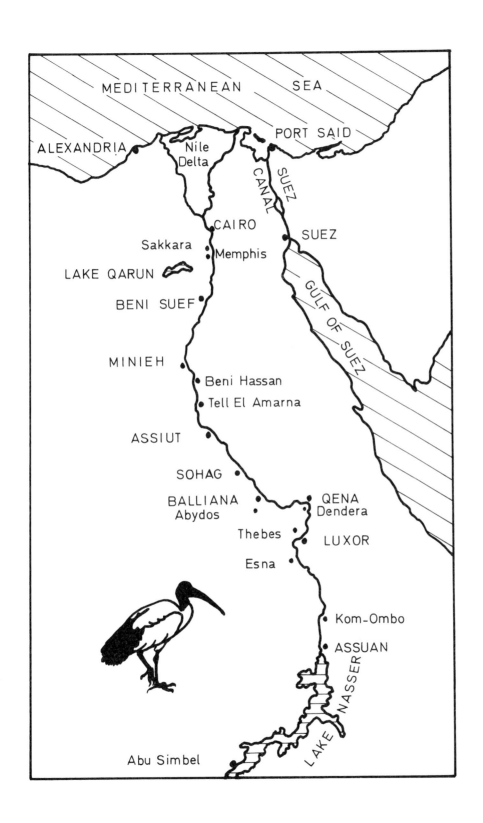

MEDITERRANEAN SEA

ALEXANDRIA

PORT SAID

Nile
Delta

SUEZ CANAL

CAIRO

SUEZ

Sakkara

Memphis

LAKE QARUN

GULF OF SUEZ

BENI SUEF

MINIEH

Beni Hassan

Tell El Amarna

ASSIUT

SOHAG

BALLIANA

QENA

Abydos

Dendera

Thebes

LUXOR

Esna

Kom-Ombo

ASSUAN

LAKE NASSER

Abu Simbel

afternoon a Hobby flew slowly over the River Nile.

Monday 28 September

A dawn walk in the fields at El Till produced rather few of even the common birds. Graceful Warbler was perhaps the best. The ride across the desert looked promising for birds, but the only one seen, a Hoopoe Lark, ran off at our approach. At El Amarna, Rock Martins were common, flickering along the cliffs above the tombs. At the Northern Palace, a Black Stork flew lazily north, and a female Desert Wheatear was seen.

Back on the Nile, we saw our first Egyptian Geese and Common Terns, and Marsh Harriers showed well, gliding over the reed beds, with at least seven being recorded.

Tuesday 29 September

The whole day was spent cruising on the Nile. Herons and egrets were common, most being too numerous to count, and 36 Egyptian Geese were recorded. Pintail and Shoveler were seen for the first time. Bird of the day was a first-year Spotted Eagle which flew over the boat as we approached the cliffs of Gebel Selin. Our only House Martin was seen amongst the flocks of European and Egyptian Swallows which overtook us as we steamed south.

As we approached Sohag road bridge, six immature Night Herons flew in and landed on an island, and a Short-toed Eagle circled over the boat as we waited to pass the bridge.

Wednesday 30 September

Sheltering in the shade at Abydos we watched a male Black-eared Wheatear feeding amongst the ruins, and a Trumpeter Finch put in a (too) brief appearance. On the journey back to the boat some of us glimpsed a Glossy Ibis and an immature Night Heron in a flooded field.

Back on the river more Night Herons were seen, and Egyptian Geese were almost commonplace. Good numbers of Squacco Herons, Garganey, Senegal Thick-knees and Blue-cheeked Bee-eaters were seen, as well as our first Black-winged Stilts.

Thursday 1 October

At Dendera we saw our only owl of the trip – a Little Owl perched on the side of one of the buildings. Rock Martins were nesting inside some of the buildings and bats were common. The walk to rejoin the boat at Khozam produced two new birds for our trip, Redstart and Olivaceous Warbler.

On the river, we had our first sighting of African Skimmers – a group of six together on a sand-bank. Other birds seen on the Nile included the now expected large numbers of herons and egrets, especially Cattle Egrets.

In the afternoon, a rather hot visit to the Valley of the Kings produced another brief sighting of Trumpeter Finches, but better views of Brown-necked Ravens, and a couple of Blue Rock Thrushes. Returning to the *Nile Star,* a Nile Valley Sunbird was seen near the ferry jetty.

Friday 2 October

A pair of Bulbuls sang regularly from a small bush beside the boat at Luxor each dawn. At the Tombs of the Nobles, a pair of Desert Larks were seen on the cliffs above, and a small flock of Black Storks circled over the hills to the west. Our first White-crowned Black Wheatears and a Masked Shrike were seen at the temple of Ramasses II, where a Green Sandpiper was flushed from a small pit. Over 30 Brown-necked Ravens were seen during the morning.

Few birds were seen during the visit to the otherwise impressive Karnak, but as we rejoined the *Nile Star* a flock of about 200 White Pelicans flew upstream in 'V' formation, giving good views to those on shore and better views still to those who had remained on the

Spur-winged Plover

boat. Black Kites were seen well when we were near the river.

Saturday 3 October

Pied Kingfishers had started to perch on the *Nile Star,* using it as a post to launch an attack of some unsuspecting fish. Eight Egyptian Geese afforded good views as they flew downstream past the *Nile Star.* At the Valley of the Queens Brown-necked Ravens and a White-crowned Black Wheatear were seen. At the Ramasseum, we found a pair of Masked Shrikes, a Graceful Warbler and the first Icterine Warblers.

We sailed from Luxor in the afternoon, spotting six Night Herons among the other herons and egrets. At dusk, a fast dark falcon flew over the Nile, giving away little of its identity – probably the closest we were to get to a Sooty Falcon.

Sunday 4 October

At dawn at Esna, Hoopoes were feeding on the bank beside the boat, and the only Tufted Ducks seen on the trip were feeding just upstream of the Barrage. Two large flocks of Spoonbills landed on an island upstream and a Hobby put in a brief appearance before we set off for the Temple of Khnum. Later that morning we sailed further upstream, and the birdwatching by now was becoming really exciting. By dusk we had seen our first Little Bittern, Ferruginous Ducks, Snipe and our only Coots of the trip, as well as over 60 Night Herons, 11 Purple Herons, over 100 Squacco Herons, 2 Glossy Ibises, 4 Ospreys and 15 Black-winged Stilts. Sadly, we also saw a dead White Stork hanging by its broken wing from a set of high tension wires which crossed the river

Monday 5 October

Dawn at Kom Ombo saw the start of probably the best day's birdwatching of the cruise. A male Little Bittern and an immature Night Heron sat among the reeds less than 50 metres from the boat. A short walk towards the village produced 5 Temminck's and 15 Little Stints amongst many other waders, but no sign of White-tailed Plover. Large flocks of Yellow Wagtails fed on the short turf at the water's edge, and Ospreys, Black Kites and Kestrels were common. Nile Valley Sunbirds were seen well and Lesser Whitethroat was seen for the first time. By breakfast the tally was

40 species.

On the move again, we sailed past sand-banks where one flock of 32 and another of 42 African Skimmers were resting. They looked quite fantastic, their enormous orange bills almost glowing in the morning sunlight. A flock of 95 Grey Herons was a surprise, since all birds we had seen so far had been either solitary or in twos and threes.

In the afternoon the visits to Elephantine and Kitchener islands were rather disappointing for birds. Previous visits there had found many birds, especially Nile Valley Sunbirds. We found our first Spotted Flycatcher, but little else. In the evening however, the 250 or more Black Kites circling over the islands were quite spectacular.

Tuesday 6 October
Those up at dawn at Assuan were rewarded with views of Green Heron. At the New High Dam, White-crowned Black Wheatears foraged on the slopes and footpaths, and Brown-necked Ravens were seen. An adult Egyptian Vulture was spotted from the bus back to Assuan. Our first White Wagtails flew over the *Nile Star* during the morning.

Those who visited Abu Simbel saw White-crowned Black-Wheatears, Brown-necked Ravens and a flock of about 50 White Storks.

In the afternoon a visit to the gardens of the Hotel Oberoi produced our first Tawny Pipit, Goldfinch and Whinchat, as well as several species of warblers we had seen previously. A flock of 51 Spoonbills flew north at dusk, as many flocks of duck flew in the opposite direction. The few ducks identified were Garganey. The Black Kites gradually increased in numbers until 250 or more circled over the islands before nightfall.

Wednesday 7 October
Sadly our last day on the Nile and our last day birdwatching. We visited Philae by boat, and it proved to be a very worthwhile trip ornithologically. Highlights were a mixed flock of 70 Black and White Storks, at least 30 Egyptian Vultures which were mainly immatures, 2 Griffon Vultures, a beautiful male Pallid Harrier, 35 Glossy Ibises and several Nile Valley Sunbirds.

Little Grebe
Levantine Shearwater
Cory's Shearwater
European Storm-Petrel
Grey Heron
Great White Egret
Little Egret   Cattle Egret
Night Heron
Spoonbill
White Stork
Teal   Shoveler
Marsh Harrier
Moorhen   Coot
Pied Avocet
Kentish Plover
Northern Lapwing
Spur-winged Plover
Curlew Sandpiper
Dunlin
Common Redshank
Common Snipe
Black-headed Gull
Little Gull   Herring Gull
Lesser Black-backed Gull
Sandwich Tern
Common Tern
Collared Dove   Palm Dove
River Kingfisher
White-breasted Kingfisher
Hoopoe
Crested Lark
Swallow
White Wagtail
Grey Wagtail
Common Bulbul
Cetti's Warbler
Graceful Warbler
Chiffchaff
Isabelline Wheatear
Orange-tufted Sunbird
House Sparrow
Magpie
Hooded Crow

Maagen Michael Fish Farm,
south of Haifa, Israel.
14 October 1986

MEDITERRANEAN SEA

Lesser Black-backed Gulls are likely to be around the ship as you sail from Port Said and enter the Mediterranean. In spring the dark-mantled Scandinavian form will be streaming north to the Baltic and northern Norway. But as you penetrate to the west they will be less evident and you will have seen the last of the White-eyed Gulls.

Generally speaking the Mediterranean carries relatively few seabirds. Its variable temperatures and high salinity make for low plankton production. There is a dearth of seabird food especially in winter. Whole populations of shearwaters, for instance, desert the Mediterranean and migrate west out to the Atlantic. Even the heavily salted water itself migrates, finding its way to the South Atlantic to balance some of the vast quantity which moves up from the Antarctic to pour into the North Atlantic ocean.

In the harbours of the eastern Mediterranean there will be gulls, and you will be exercised in putting names to some of them, a fact which the vast majority of ocean travellers find astonishing. One of the commonest remarks overheard on any ship's deck where people are vaguely birdwatching is, 'Oh, they're just seagulls', as if they were of no significance, rather in the way people dismiss pigeons and ducks in a public park, as being 'un-birds'. Commonly there will be Black-headed, Mediterranean, Herring and Little Gulls in evidence, but that doesn't begin to hint at the complexity of forms and age-plumages which are sent to confuse us. The

common or garden Herring Gull which we all know and love as the archetypal British 'seagull' is replaced in the Mediterranean by a yellow-legged race which is accepted by the rest of the world as a full species *Larus cachinnans.* The Yellow-legged Gull, apart from yellow legs, has a darker mantle than our pink-legged version. To further confuse the issue there is yet a third race/species, the Armenian Gull, which breeds in Armenia and Turkey but winters across on the North African coast.

If you get to the wonderful fish ponds at Maagen Michael, South of Haifa in Israel, before the end of March, you may see the Great Black-headed Gulls which winter there. There will also be a host of waders, many of them remarkably tame. The Night Herons perch on top of the netting which protects some of the fish-breeding ponds from their depredations, along with egrets and White Storks. On their migrations the storks concentrate where feeding is good, as on the marshy ground near the Maagan Michael fish ponds. They wait at the roost-place only long enough for the sun to provide warmth and lift before passing overhead in tens of thousands in a day. Those overflying the eastern Mediterranean will have wintered in South and East Africa. Funnelling up the Red Sea they are on their way to the rooftops of Poland and Eastern Europe.

Cyprus is one of the ornithological hot-spots of the whole Mediterranean, balanced neatly by Majorca at the other end of the sea. Although this beautiful island is marred by the unfortunate prevalence of small-bird hunting, there are many good things to see. Glossy Ibises, Red-footed Falcons, Lesser Kestrels, Demoiselle

Griffon Vulture
Eleanora's Falcon
Red-footed Falcon
Common Kestrel
Lapwing
River Kingfisher
Crested Lark
Red-throated Pipit
White Wagtail
Yellow Wagtail
Fan-tailed Warbler
Cyprus Warbler
Stonechat
Great Tit
Blue Tit
Goldfinch
Spanish Sparrow
Hooded Crow
Jackdaw

Limassol and Akrotiri, Cyprus.
13 October 1986

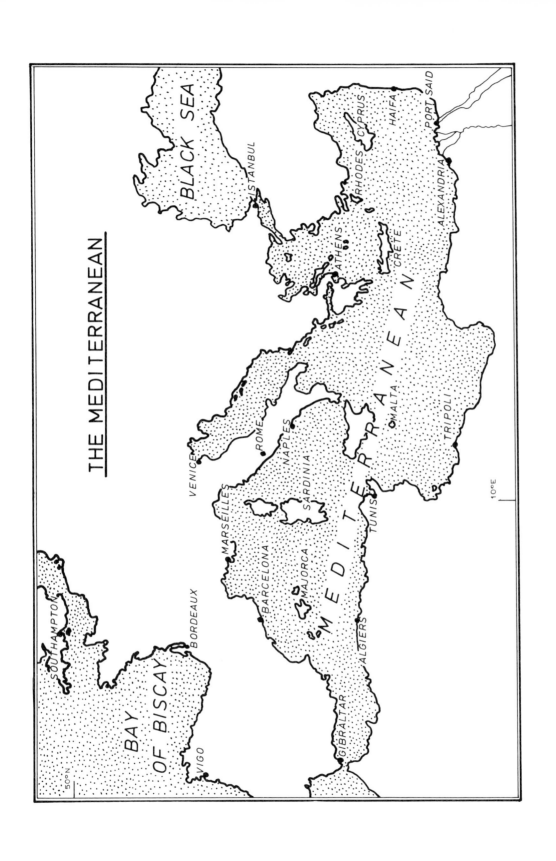

THE MEDITERRANEAN

BLACK SEA

ISTANBUL

RHODES
CYPRUS
HAIFA
PORT SAID

ATHENS
ALEXANDRIA
CRETE

M E D I T E R R A N E A N

VENICE
ROME
NAPLES
SARDINIA
MALTA
TRIPOLI

MARSEILLES
BARCELONA
MAJORCA
TUNIS
ALGIERS

10°E

BAY
OF BISCAY

SOUTHAMPTON
BORDEAUX
GIBRALTAR
VIGO

50°N

Left: *Balearic race of the Manx Shearwater;* right: *Cory's Shearwater. Their breeding range overlaps in the western Mediterranean, but Cory's is a much larger and heavier-looking bird. It is also a more enthusiastic ship-follower*

Sparrowhawk
Golden Eagle
Common Kestrel
Black-headed Gull
Feral Pigeon
Collared Dove
Crag Martin
River Kingfisher
Blackcap
Sardinian Warbler
Willow Warbler
Stonechat
Blue Rock Thrush
Black-eared Wheatear
Redstart
Coal Tit
Great Tit
Blue Tit
Rock Nuthatch
Short-toed Treecreeper
Cirl Bunting
Chaffinch
Goldfinch
Greenfinch
Tree Sparrow
Magpie
Alpine Chough
Raven
Hooded Crow

Itea and Delphi, Greece.
17 October 1986

Cranes, Little Stints, Marsh and Wood Sandpipers are just a few of the long list of goodies. On the coast at Akrotiri, just a short distance from Limassol harbour, there are Griffon Vultures and a colony of Eleonora's Falcons. These graceful little falcons are migratory, returning to the cliffs here late in April, after wintering in Madagascar and south-east Africa. They breed rather late in the year in order to have their chicks at the right age to take advantage of the passing hordes of tired migrant songbirds in autumn.

The Aegean Sea represents the world headquarters for both Eleonora's Falcon and for the local race of the impressive Cory's Shearwater, with its yellow-coloured bill. If you're lucky, you might run into flocks of hundreds, settled on the surface of the sea, only to be disturbed by the passing of your ship to fly off stiffly in a flight which is deceptively languid. Manx Shearwaters appear in two guises in this sea: at the western end the Balearic race *Puffinus p. mauretanicus* and in the central and eastern end the Levantine *P.p. yelkouan.* Apparently yelkouan is a Turkish name which has been loosely translated as 'lost soul of early Christian looking for

Above:
The Captain's deck towards sundown. Bernard Watts leans on the rail in anticipation of the departure of the sun-worshippers and the arrival of roosting songbirds
TONY SOPER

Right:
In this potted Umbrella Tree there are three roosting Lesser Whitethroats and one Blackcap
TONY SOPER

Venice
In Venice, as well as the Italian Sparrows and Feral Pigeons in St Marks Square, look out for Little Egrets on the mud banks and islands. Black, Common, Whiskered and Little Terns hunt the watery margins.

a place to rest', a neat reference to the seemingly endless travels of the wave-riding shearwater.

Because of the Mediterranean's high salinity and low food production in winter, shearwaters migrate westwards then. The Levantine birds appear to go no further than the waters off Gibraltar, while the Balearic form ventures out to the open Atlantic. Cory's Shearwaters winter in South Africa and apparently there is a possibility that some hardy or adventurous or lost individuals return north by way of the 'wrong' ocean, re-entering the Mediterranean by way of the Red Sea.

If the Mediterranean is a slightly disappointing sea for seabirds it can make up for it by being excellent for migrating landbirds which use a ship for resting purposes. In April, on passage through this sea, we recorded a lot of small birds. While passengers sunned themselves in deck-chairs, the wagtails hawked for moths and butterflies. A Robin fluttered about the funnels, a Nightingale knocked itself out on a window and Blackcaps fed on biscuit crumbs. As the light began to fail in the evening, Lesser Whitethroats would jockey for the best roosting-corner under a pile of stacked deck-chairs. At dawn we would make a sad patrol, collecting the

Home to Roost
Birds which roosted in the Weeping Fig or the Umbrella Tree on the Captain's deck of *Canberra*, between the Red Sea and Palma, Majorca.
3–10 April 1988

3 April Yellow Wagtail
7 April Lesser Whitethroat
7 April Blackcap
7 April Willow Warbler
7 April Chiffchaff
8 April Wood Warbler
10 April Spectacled Warbler
10 April Subalpine Warbler

Common Swifts
Alpine Swifts
Blackcap
Chaffinch
House Sparrow
Serin
Blackbird
Grey Wagtail
Sandwich Tern
Mediterranean Gull
Black-headed Gull
Herring Gull
Blue Tit
Great Tit
Wren
Willow Warbler
Wood Warbler
Tree Sparrow
Jackdaw
Robin

Naples. 9 April 1988

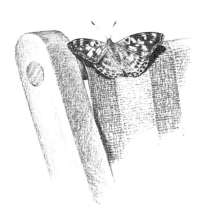

Painted Lady butterflies cover great distances on migration. Like cross-ocean landbirds they may rest on ships in large numbers

fluffy bundles which hadn't survived the night, but many more birds picked up strength with the sun, fed on insects and crumbs and flew on. Ospreys, Kestrels and Squacco Herons overflew us without stopping. A Turtle Dove kept station with us for five minutes before leaving to fly off to the north. Another Turtle Dove tried to land on a radio aerial, but thought better of it. And then we had our best bird of the day when a male Cretzschmar's Bunting turned up on 'A' deck aft, by the swimming pool. Hopping about the deck-chairs, it almost perched on my foot as it passed by while we took its photograph. Then, as we closed the toe of Italy all birds left the ship at 5.30 in the afternoon, and all was quiet.

From our berth in Naples docks we could see Common and Alpine Swifts. During the day Sandwich Terns, Mediterranean, Black-headed and Herring Gulls, Blackcaps and Serins passed by. Next day, at sea, the songbirds began to come aboard again.

I have already mentioned three potted bushes which, left over from an official beano in Sydney, decorated the Captain's deck on *Canberra* and provided shelter for roosting wagtails in the Red Sea (see p126). Two were Weeping Figs and the third an Umbrella Tree. They offered a leafy dell for resting migrants and for the whole of the Mediterranean passage we monitored their inhabitants each night. One of the attractions, of course, was that this green oasis also attracted flying insects which were enthusiastically picked off by the birds. On the tenth of April we had single specimens of Willow, Spectacled and Subalpine Warbler wandering the decks, to our joy. The last two rounded off their performance by going to the bushes to sleep.

In the morning they had gone. But now we had Cory's and Balearic Shearwaters to keep us company, along with the Yellow-legged Herring Gulls which followed in our wake. Some fifteen thousand pairs of the gulls breed in the Spanish Mediterranean, they are the most regularly seen birds at sea. They are increasing, whereas the Balearic Shearwaters are significantly less common than they once were, with perhaps less than five thousand pairs breeding in the sea-caves of the Balearics. Cory's outnumber them and there may be ten thousand pairs in both the Balearic and Columbretes Islands.

The best time for Majorca, a birder's paradise, is late April and May, when the spring migrants peak. And the charming and relatively unspoiled town of Puerto Pollensa is the place to make for. In the newly designated official reserve of Albufeira marsh there are four thousand acres of tamarisk scrub, lagoons and canals plus some old salt pans. Well protected by the Spanish guardians, there are egrets, herons, harriers, osprey, ducks and songbirds, and the visit can easily be worked into a day ashore.

Among the Yellow-legged Herring Gulls in Palma Harbour you may well find Audouin's Gull. More the size of a Mew Gull, it has slender wings, a blood-red beak and dark legs, and picks food from the water most delicately. At one time it was believed to be endangered. Still uncommon, with less than a thousand pairs breeding in the Spanish Mediterranean, it breeds colonially on flat islets, a trait which made its eggs easy to exploit in the past. But now, with a measure of protection, it is increasing.

Painted Lady butterflies may arrive to decorate a ship in thousands, resting on their way across the sea to Spain and France. If they seem to need help you may offer them sugar-water in this classic recipe. Half a teaspoon of honey and half a teaspoon of castor sugar to a breakfast cup of water. This may seem a weak mixture but although the insects will eagerly attack a stronger solution it will upset their digestion and shorten life. Put some of the mix in a saucer and create a cotton-wool island. Introduce a butterfly to the island and it will unroll its tongue and suck the moisture. If it is really exhausted it may be necessary to use a pin or needle to uncoil the tongue, gently drawing it out and touching it to the damp cotton wool.

Though you may get some personal satisfaction in succouring the butterfly or the exhausted bird, the truth is that the landbirds and insects seen on board represent a totally insignificant sample of the massive numbers which are passing overhead, often in the hours of darkness. On a dark night, incidentally, there may be hordes of luminescent jellyfish to light the sea with globes of fire.

Unlike the situation further east, the approaches and the Straits of Gibraltar involve some lively mixing of currents, so there is good feeding all year round. Storm-petrels and skuas join the shearwaters, there may be Razorbills and puffins as well as a good spread of gulls and terns. And as you turn the corner into the Atlantic, Northern Gannets welcome you back and the Herring Gulls sport pink legs.

Place of Rest
Passage birds using *Canberra* as a temporary hotel during passage of the Mediterranean, 7–10 April 1988 (in order of arrival)

Blackcap
Lesser Whitethroat
Tree Pipit
Black-headed Yellow Wagtail
Common Whitethroat
Willow Warbler
White Wagtail
Robin
Song Thrush
Nightingale
Wheatear
Chiffchaff
Corn Bunting
Redstart
Cretzschmar's Bunting
Wood Warbler
Spectacled Warbler
Subalpine Warbler

NORTH SEA, NORWEGIAN SEA

The familiar 'pink-legged British' Herring Gulls and possibly the odd Mew Gull follow in your wake as you sail from a Channel port and head into the North Sea which, like most of the others, is not so much species-rich as rich in numbers. A small and shallow sea, it nevertheless enjoys currents and a turbulence which nourish the plankton which in turn feed fish and several million seabirds; all in spite of the pollution which defiles it but *may* be on the verge of defeat.

Unlike other seas and oceans, its bird-list seems reasonably constant no matter which port you sail from. There is not that steady progression of 'new' birds which makes an Atlantic or Pacific cruise such a delight. But once well away from land there will be Black-legged Kittiwakes and Northern Gannets and the nearest thing we see to an albatross in these waters – the Northern Fulmar. In fact it is not strictly true to say that you have no chance of an albatross, for there have been well over a dozen British and Irish sightings within the last thirty years, most of them the Black-browed. These have been birds which, one way or another, have conquered the flight problems of the windless doldrums and ended up in the 'wrong' hemisphere. One Black-browed Albatross lived with the gannet colony on the Bass Rock for four months, in which time it was seen and photographed many times. Another took up residence in Iceland and yet another at Hermaness, Shetland, in a gannet colony. It obviously thought it was a gannet as it

Opposite:
The Northern Fulmar looks superficially like a largish bull-necked gull, but is a tube-nose. Over the last hundred years they have flourished mightily and extended their breeding range in both the North Pacific and Atlantic
MARTIN WITHERS/FLPA

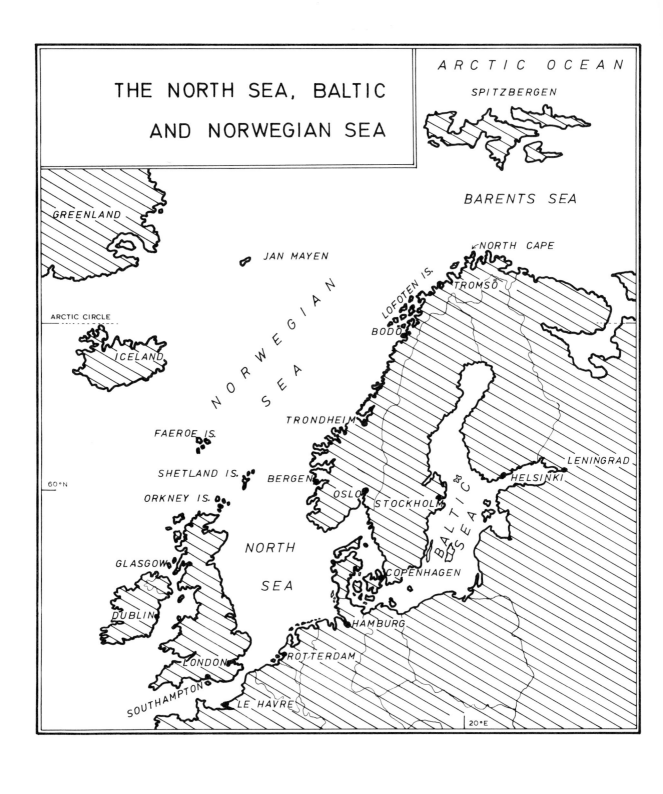

THE NORTH SEA, BALTIC AND NORWEGIAN SEA

ARCTIC OCEAN

SPITZBERGEN

GREENLAND

BARENTS SEA

JAN MAYEN

NORTH CAPE

LOFOTEN IS.

TROMSØ

ARCTIC CIRCLE

BODØ

ICELAND

N O R W E G I A N   S E A

TRONDHEIM

FAEROE IS.

LENINGRAD

HELSINKI

60°N

SHETLAND IS.

BERGEN

OSLO

STOCKHOLM

ORKNEY IS.

B
A
L
T
I
C

S
E
A

NORTH

GLASGOW

SEA

COPENHAGEN

DUBLIN

HAMBURG

LONDON

ROTTERDAM

SOUTHAMPTON

LE HAVRE

20°E

turned up annually between February and August for several years – certainly until 1987.

If your chance of an albatross is small, you will certainly see the stiff-winged fulmars and the persil-white gannets every day on passage through the North Sea. There will be auks, too, especially in midsummer when the breeding-cliffs are alive with hungry chicks and the parents are out at sea fishing. Professional submersible pilots, working in connection with the oil exploration companies, have actually seen Razorbills at a depth of 460ft (140m), actively swimming. This is greater than the maximum depth of Razorbills trapped and drowned in bottom-set fishing nets when they have been recorded at 394ft (120m). Guillemots regularly achieve 590ft (180m) but Atlantic Puffins apparently have not been found below 197ft (60m).

The oil-rigs which are such a feature of the northern North Sea provide welcome resting-places for migratory birds like pipits,

Great Crested Grebe
Northern Fulmar
Manx Shearwater
Northern Gannet
Shag
Grey Heron
Common Eider
Red-breasted Merganser
Goosander
White-tailed Sea Eagle
Rough-legged Buzzard
Hen Harrier
Oystercatcher
Lapwing
Golden Plover
Snipe
Whimbrel
Wood Sandpiper
Hooded Crow
Willow Tit
Dipper
Fieldfare
Redwing
Wheatear
Whinchat
Redstart
Red-spotted Bluethroat
Icterine Warbler
Blackcap
Willow Warbler
Chiffchaff
Spotted Flycatcher
Tree Pipit
Rock Pipit
White Wagtail
Twite
Brambling

Southampton–North Cape, Norway.
4–18 July 1984

Guillemots fly underwater, using their wings in chasing small fish, their feet as control surfaces

147

The 'sea-swallows' breed from temperate latitudes to the edge of the Arctic ice, farther north than any other tern. Outside the nesting season they are almost entirely marine, though they will rest on anything from a floating tree-trunk to an ice-floe. On migration they commute almost from pole to pole, covering a greater mileage and enjoying more daylight in their lives than any other bird

finches and starlings. And in turn they are patronised by migratory birds of prey which take advantage of the facilities for refuelling! Short-eared Owls, especially, are common passage birds at oil-rigs, where they prey on the songbirds.

Once clear of British latitudes and entering the Norwegian Sea there is a marked increase in bird activity and a better chance of seeing whales, which are not uncommon passing on their way from the open Atlantic to the Arctic. Orcas (Killer Whales) and Bottle-nosed are the most frequently seen, as well as the Pilot Whales which are the subject of a controversial fishery in the Faeroes. They are highly sociable, travelling in groups of maybe several hundred, easily identified by the bulging 'pot-head'.

Cruising the Norwegian fjords there will be Arctic Terns, Black-headed Gulls, Red-breasted Mergansers and Eiders. But the flesh-legged Herring Gulls of British waters will now appear in the yellow-legged form *L.a. argentatus* . And the Lesser Black-backed

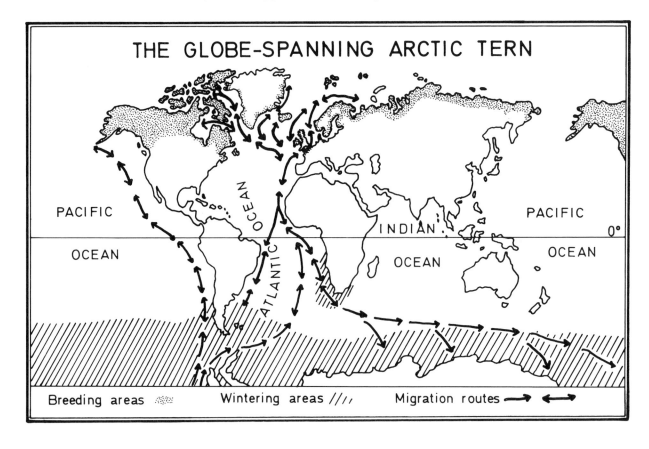

THE GLOBE-SPANNING ARCTIC TERN

PACIFIC OCEAN

PACIFIC OCEAN

ATLANTIC OCEAN

INDIAN OCEAN

0°

Breeding areas ········· Wintering areas //// Migration routes ⟶ ⟷

Gulls of Norway and the Baltic are the dark-mantled Scandinavian *Larus fuscus fuscus* , with bright yellow legs to help distinguish them from the larger pink-legged Great Black-backed Gull.

The further north you go the greater is the proportion of dark-phase 'blue' fulmars amongst the Northern Fulmars which are so much a part of the sea-going scene. And on shore the conifer forests are reluctant to give way to tundra because of the influence of the warm North Atlantic current bequeathed by the tropical Gulf Stream. Even as far north as Trondheim the landscape is dominated by conifer hills overlooking lakes. But there is a first-class marsh sanctuary at Fokstumyra not too far away. A breeding-place for many waders and wildfowl, with cranes and raptors for good measure. Ruff, Whimbrel, Hen Harrier and Short-eared Owls are here, but the cream of the reserve is the strong probability of seeing Red-spotted Bluethroats in glorious technicolour, perched in the willow scrub.

North of the Arctic Circle, which is marked on the mainland side of the sheltered passage by a globe-shaped symbol, you might expect the land to be sheathed in ice, but again the influence of the warm currents prevails. In the breeding season the shoreline and harbours hereabouts are noisy with terns, Arctic Terns, appropriately. While these globe-spanners breed in small numbers even as far south as the Isle of Aran and Ayrshire in Scotland, they are typically high Arctic birds, breeding on top of the world to travel 11,000 miles (17,700km) to high southern latitudes to 'winter', then working their way back up the seaboard of South America and West Africa to skirt Western Europe and return to the Arctic, a round-trip 22,000 miles (35,400km) a year, rewarding them with a life of perpetual summer.

South of the Lofoten Islands lies the island of Røst, home of a famous puffinry. Hereabouts there will be many Atlantic Puffins at sea. And in the seaport of Leknes – a puffin dog. These dogs, existing now only as show specimens, have a modified claw which is said to make them excel at climbing. This, with an extra soft mouth, fitted them for their rôle as puffin-collectors. In the old days these dogs were trained to go into the burrow to extract the adult bird, then return to fetch out the egg. The Norwegian Puffin-dog Club was allegedly formed in 1550, which must surely qualify it for the *Guinness Book of Records*.

White-tailed Sea Eagles have declined in numbers along the coast of Norway as a consequence of persecution. Protected nowadays and possibly increasing locally

Gannets

Northern – North Atlantic
Australasian –
     Southern Australia and New Zealand
Cape – South Africa

Gannets join with boobies to form the family *Sulidae.* They are plunge-divers, double breasted to absorb impact with the sea. Their bodies are cigar shaped and they have long fairly narrow wings, wedge-shaped tails, stout bills and forward-facing eyes. The three gannet species are physically very similar, though the Northern is slightly larger, fitting it for the more rigorous conditions it faces. And while the Northern Gannet is a cliff-nester, the African Cape Gannet and Australasian Gannet nest on the flat ground.

The Northern Gannet *Sula bassana is* the largest and most spectacular of North Atlantic seabirds. 'Whiter than white' at a distance, 'pointed at both ends' when close,

Gulls

Pacific
Kelp
Black-tailed
Western
Slaty-backed
Herring
Lesser Black-backed
Great Black-backed
Heermann's
Thayer's
California
Ring-billed
Mew
Sabine's
Glaucous
Iceland
Kumlien's

Ivory
Black-headed
Bonaparte's
Little
Laughing
Franklin's
Glaucous-winged
Black-billed
Silver
Grey-headed
Swallow-tailed
Lava
Andean
Grey
Band-tailed
Dolphin
Indian Black-headed

Relict
Chinese
   Black-headed
Brown-hooded
Mediterranean
Slender-billed
Audouin's

White-eyed
Sooty
Great Black-headed
Black-legged Kittiwake
Red-legged Kittiwake
Ross's

Most gulls are birds of the northern hemisphere, though some are found way down in the Southern Ocean. They are moderate to large in size, varying in length from about 12 to 30in (30 to 75cm). They are more or less white as adults, more or less grey as

conspicuous black wing-tips, 6ft (1.8m) wing-span, powerful flight. It attains full adult plumage in its fourth year. Vertical plunge-dives from as much as a 100ft (30m), but more usually 30ft (9m), in pursuit of fast pelagic fish like mackerel. Unlike boobies, gannets may roost at sea, congregating in rafts. Highly gregarious, breeding on remote islands and undisturbed cliffs of the Gulf of St Lawrence, Newfoundland, Labrador, Iceland, France, and more recently Norway, but the main stations are along the west coast of Britain and Ireland, where seventeen colonies hold over 70 per cent of the world population. After a disastrous decline in the nineteenth century as a result of persecution, they enjoyed a general increase in the twentieth century. Only one British gannetry, at Sula Sgeir, is still legally raided for the fat 'gugas', which were once commonly eaten at Scottish banquets as 'a most delicate fowle'.

Northern gannets range the North Atlantic, overlapping in Florida and the Caribbean with the Masked Booby, to cause confusion, and perhaps as far as southern Africa, to be confused with the Cape Gannet.

juveniles but they offer the supreme challenge in field identification in that they are comparatively uniform in colouration and carriage yet present a seemingly infinite range of subtle variations in plumage. To make matters worse, they may hybridise or wear the white coat of an albino. They are supremely adapted to breeding requirements, nesting anywhere from the Arctic pack-ice to exposed cliffs or seaside rooftops. They are opportunist feeders, mainly scavengers, enjoying ship's garbage, rubbish dumps, sewer outfalls and lunchtime crusts in the city park. Sociable in feeding and at the nest colony, they will even nest happily in company with other species such as terns or auks. Though they are barely tolerated by some people, they have a high resistance to persecution and their numbers are generally increasing.

Great Crested Grebe
Slavonian Grebe
Little Grebe
Northern Fulmar
Northern Gannet
Great Cormorant
Mute Swan
Greylag
Shelduck
Mallard
Tufted Duck
Eider
Velvet Scoter
Goosander
Red-breasted Merganser
Sparrowhawk
Pheasant
Common Crane
Coot
Oystercatcher
Pied Avocet
Ringed Plover
Ruddy Turnstone
Lapwing
Redshank
Spotted Redshank
Greenshank
Common Sandpiper
Green Sandpiper
Wood Sandpiper
Great Skua
Arctic Skua
Black-headed Gull
Herring Gull
Lesser Black-backed Gull
Great Black-backed Gull
Mew Gull
Sandwich Tern
Common Tern
Arctic Tern
Little Tern
Razorbill
Black Guillemot
Feral Pigeon
Woodpigeon
Cuckoo

continued opposite

The Lofotens are beautiful islands with a diversity of habitats from sheer cliffs and mountains to sheltered bays and sandy beaches. Take a coastal tripper-boat for the day and as well as auks and eiders you will see one of the strongholds of the White-tailed Sea Eagle. These superb coastal eagles are relatively abundant along the wild cliffs of northern Norway, making their eyries on ledges which are often scenically well chosen but too easy of access. In the past, they have been much persecuted, as birds of prey so often have been, by farmers and hunters ignorant of their value in regulating other animal populations.

With luck you will see several sea eagles as you work the coast from Leknes. On one memorable afternoon we ate a picnic lunch in an idyllic natural harbour with Black Guillemots and Eiders watching from a discreet distance and a young eagle glowering at us from a rocky islet just a couple of hundred feet away. There is one record of an enterprising pair of sea eagles which took over the top of a navigation beacon to build their nest of seaweed and driftwood with an inner lining of heather and moss.

A newly established gannetry on the island of Hovsflesa shares one of the low skerries with a colony of Great Cormorants. Since 1974 the gannets have been slowly increasing in numbers, in line with the general increase in the population of Northern Gannets. Herrings, and to a lesser extent Mackerel and Coalfish, are their main prey, but further north and into Finnmark, the shoals of Capelin fuel the expansion of gannetries. The colder water of the Norwegian Sea supports generally larger numbers of fulmars, auks, skuas and shearwaters as well as gannets.

All four skuas (jaegers) may be seen in fair numbers as passage birds in spring and autumn, and they will also be seen, but not so commonly, in the summer. Great and Arctic Skuas breed from Shetland northwards, the Pomarine and Long-tailed are more typical of the high Arctic. At sea the Long-tailed Skuas seem most in evidence. Glaucous Gulls begin to be a possibility in these latitudes, with their fierce expressions and white wings.

Approaching the North Cape you pass several sensational bird islands, among them Hjelmsøy with its thousands of Atlantic Puffins. If the weather is quiet enough the pilot may be persuaded to close within a few cables of the sheer cliffs, with their massed ranks of Black-legged Kittiwakes fringed by Shags at the base. And

Arctic Tern feeding chick

Swift
Black Woodpecker
Skylark Swallow
Sand Martin
House Martin
Tree Pipit Meadow Pipit
White Wagtail
Reed Warbler
Marsh Warbler
Sedge Warbler
Whitethroat
Lesser Whitethroat
Garden Warbler
Blackcap
Willow Warbler
Wood Warbler
Goldcrest
Spotted Flycatcher
Pied Flycatcher
Wheatear
Blackbird
Fieldfare
Redwing
Song Thrush
Willow Tit
Blue Tit Great Tit
Treecreeper
Wren
Yellowhammer
Reed Bunting
Chaffinch Greenfinch
Siskin
Parrot Crossbill
House Sparrow
Starling
Jay Magpie
Raven
Hooded Crow
Jackdaw

*Baltic Cruise. Southampton
– Travëmunde – Helsinki –
Leningrad – Stockholm –
Copenhagen – Oslo –
Southampton.
1–15 July 1986*

the water will be crowded with off-duty auks and fishing terns. The Common Guillemots (murres) in these northern waters have black upperparts in place of the more southern chocolate.

At the North Cape itself, the anchorage is off a Lapp fishing settlement called Skarsvag, a remote and treeless place, backed by a tundra plateau characterised by dwarf willows and home to Arctic Golden Plovers and Long-tailed Skuas. Terns will be fishing here, Eiders and Atlantic Puffins as well. On the freshwater lakes there are Red-breasted Mergansers and you just might see a well-placed reindeer on your way to the official North Cape lookout. Here at 71° 10' North the sun is well above the northern horizon at midnight in high summer and you gaze across the Barents Sea to the distant Arctic Ocean. Behind your back is the souvenir shop and café with a long multiracial queue. But on one memorable occasion the crew of P&O's *Sea Princess* ferried an upright piano ashore and lugged it up to the edge of the cliff, where classical pianist John Briggs ravished his Arctic audience with the inevitable selection of Grieg's greatest hits. The North Cape is an experience.

In ornithological terms, the best is yet to come if you are lucky enough to penetrate further north, first past Bear Island, where ten thousand of the Arctic Little Auks breed, and then on to

Spitzbergen, with its spectacular congregation of breeding sea-birds. Even here at 80⁰ North the Gulf Stream has bequeathed its influence; the warm west-wind current creeping between Scotland and Iceland keeps the sea ice-free in summer. At the equivalent latitude in the Southern Hemisphere, 80⁰ South, there is a frozen wilderness, but here is a welcoming island with flowering plants and mosses, vast numbers of breeding fulmars

Terms

Whiskered	Bridled
White-winged Black	Sooty
Black	Fairy
Large-billed	Black-fronted
Gull-billed	Amazon
Caspian	Damara
Indian River	Peruvian
South American	Little
Common	Crested
Arctic	Royal
Antarctic	Lesser Crested
Kerguelen	Chinese Crested
Forster's	Cayenne
Trudeau's	Elegant
Roseate	Sandwich
White-fronted	Inca
White-cheeked	White
Black-naped	Grey Noddy
Black-bellied	Brown Noddy
Aleutian	Lesser Noddy
Grey-backed	Black Noddy

There are over forty species of tern, from the Arctic to the Antarctic. Most are birds of the coast, some are oceanic. They are smaller, more graceful and more stream-lined than the gulls which they superficially resemble, but they have narrower, more pointed wings and slender, sharp-pointed bills. Many have deeply forked tails, earning them the sailor's name of sea-swallow. They are short in the legs with small webbed feet buoyant on the sea yet rarely in it, for they swim poorly. They often enjoy a rest on a piece of driftwood or raft of seaweed.

They tend to have white bodies with grey backs and wings, very often a black cap and sometimes a jaunty crest. Their bills and feet range in colour from black to blood-red or yellow. Exceptionally aerial, they roost at night but are in the air for most of the day, outside the breeding season. They can live for long periods on the wing. They fly with steady, purposeful wing-beats, never soaring, tending to look down, their beaks pointing to the water. In searching for fish they may hover, then plunge head first for small fish at the surface – splash, snatch and up again.

They will normally have paired before they reach the nesting quarters but courting

and skuas, auks and terns. Glaucous, Ivory and Sabine's Gulls are found here, and the far northern Brünnich's Guillemot.

Little Auks crowd the sea-cliff crevices, oceanic birds which come ashore to breed in this unlikely spot. Just 8in (20cm) overall, they have dumpy bodies, well covered in fat to withstand the Arctic cold, and even their bills are shortened to reduce heat loss and keep their internal fires stoked. On the sea these tubby little birds

continues with highly ritualised displays which include ceremonial feeding. Typically, terns nest in close-packed colonies, some of them very populous indeed. The stimulus and noise of company leads them to synchronise their egg-laying, with resulting advantages in terms of safety – the safety of numbers which confuses predators. Even so, there is high mortality, which accounts for the average clutch of three or four eggs in many species as against the single egg of, for instance, the Sooty Tern, which suffers less from predation.

The nest is often little more than a shallow depression, a hollow on a sandy or shingle beach, usually on an island. The chicks are fed on whole small fish, such as sand-eels, which may be longer than the chick itself, so that while the head end is being digested the tail hangs out for all to see.

Breeding success is heavily dependent on the supply of suitable fish and sometimes a particularly high tide will create havoc. Predators like rats, skuas, gulls, crows and owls take a heavy toll. The chicks are heavily dependent on their parents until long after they have fledged, but if they are lucky they may live to the ripe old age of thirty.

almost seem to lack necks as well as beaks, they are so well wrapped against the cold. But there is method in their madness, for close to the pack-ice the plankton is thick and rich. Royal Navy submarines have even seen Little Auks through their periscopes while submerged, 'flying' underwater through a soup of fish and jellyfish and plankton. In wintertime the Little Auks disperse to the Norwegian sea and even to the northernmost parts of the British Isles. Like storm-petrels, they may on occasion be overwhelmed by high winds and 'wrecked' ashore.

Glaucous Gulls are increasing in numbers here, as is another circumpolar species, Sabine's Gull. Only one other gull in the world has a forked tail, the Swallow-tailed, and as that breeds almost exclusively on the equatorial Galapagos Islands there's not much chance of confusing them in these high Arctic latitudes. But

Little Auks are birds of the Arctic Ocean, well cushioned with fat
MARTIN B. WITHERS/FLPA

in winter Sabine's ranges down to South Africa by way of north-west Europe, while the Canadian and Alaskan Arctic birds reach the South Pacific coast as far as Peru, where they may overlap with their Galapagos cousins.

The delicately patterned Ross's Gull, which must be one of the 'most-wanted' of all gulls for anyone's list, breeds on Spitzbergen. And, most Arctic of all species, the Ivory Gull not only breeds here but stays for the dark half of the year, haunting the pack-ice to scavenge a living at the very edge of the permanent ice which covers the roof of the world. Most of the teeming masses of birds which breed here visit only during the brief but plentiful weeks of high summer, just as most visiting ships choose the time of the midnight sun. But if, at that time, you are lucky enough to penetrate as far as the ice, then there will be Northern Fulmars, Arctic Skuas, Brünnich's and Black Guillemots and Little Auks exploring the leads with you as well as kittiwakes and the other fabled gulls.

Brünnich's Guillemots breed in the high Arctic at the time of the midnight sun
ERIC& DAVID HOSKING

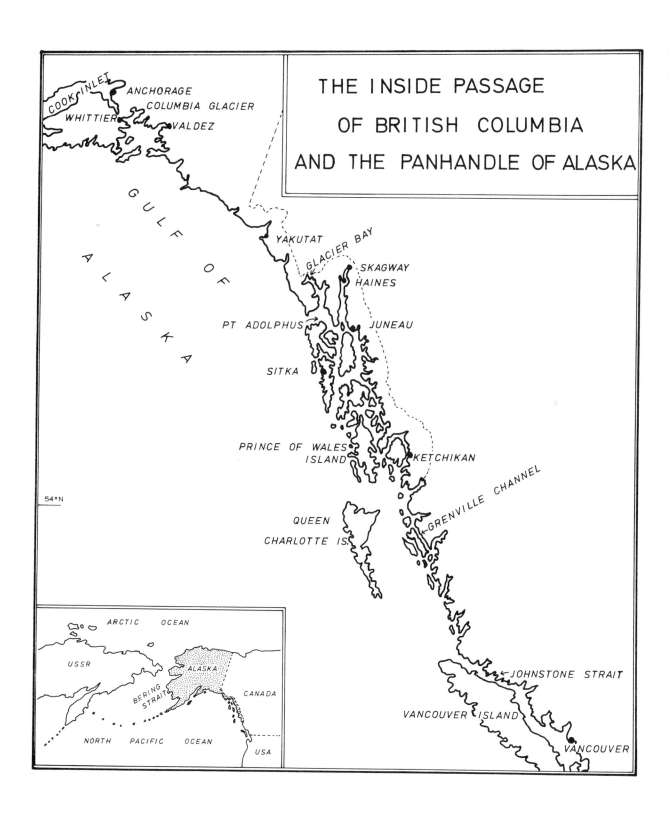

THE INSIDE PASSAGE
British Columbia and Alaska

The voyage through the Inside Passage from Vancouver in British Columbia to Glacier Bay in the northern part of the Alaskan panhandle offers the finest scenic panorama to be seen from the deck of an ocean-going ship. Where the placid waters of the Pacific drown the valleys of the Coast Range, vivid green forests flank snow-clad peaks which rear aloft in sublime grandeur. Broad bays lead to mountain-locked inlets and awesome tide-water glaciers. Narrow channels, swept by fearsome currents, wind between spruce-tufted islands. Bald Eagles survey their kingdom and Glaucous-winged Gulls follow your ship for galley waste.

Sailing from Vancouver, any midsummer passage north through the sheltered waterway is programmed for a birder's delight. On the pierside sheds at Ballantyne Pier there will be dozens of Glaucous-winged Gulls nesting on the flat roofs. In the beginning of July there will still be some sitting on eggs while the young chicks of other pairs begin to explore their surroundings. Reaching under the Lions Gate Bridge there will be Double-crested and Pelagic Cormorants nesting colonially on ledges in the sheer rock face on your port hand. As they flight home past the ship after fishing expeditions you can see the slender, straight-stretched neck of the Pelagic as compared with the distinctly kinked neck of the Double-crested.

The Glaucous-winged Gulls are abundant along this coast, they

Glaucous-winged Gull
Double-crested Cormorant
Pelagic Cormorant
Surf Scoter
Dall's Porpoise
Marbled Murrelet
Common Murre
Bald Eagle
Rhinoceros Auklet
Rufous Hummingbird
Pigeon Guillemot
Orca
Mew Gull

Sailing north from Vancouver, British Columbia 4 July 1988

Rhinoceros Auklet

Opposite:
*Glaucous-winged Gulls
follow ships through the
Inside Passage*
TONY SOPER

Below:
*Check the treetops for Bald
Eagles, whose snow-white
heads become conspicuous
once you 'get your eye in'*
TONY SOPER

enjoy the benefits of human settlements and the bounty which spews from ships and boats, so you can be sure of their constant company. For European visitors, the numerous Mew (Common) Gulls are also a pleasure, for the proportions of Mews to Herring Gulls are neatly reversed from those to which Europeans are accustomed. Tufted Puffins may appear at any time.

The open straits which separate the mainland from Vancouver Island are home to many whales in summer. About fifty Gray Whales are found on the Pacific Coast of the island, where they

Bald Eagles
Rufous Hummingbird (on
ship's rail)
Red-necked Phalarope
Common Loon
Humpback Whale
Dall's Porpoises
Black Scoter
Pomarine Jaeger
Common Murre
Marbled Murrelet
Tufted Puffin

Ketchikan, Alaska.
5 July 1988

feed after their winter fast in the waters off Baja California. Along the inside passage, many more are passage migrants on their way to the Bering Sea.

Bowhead Whales mate in these waters. Minke and Orcas (Killer Whales) move here from the open Pacific to spend the summer, along with Sei, a few Pacific Right Whales and more Humpbacks. The Orcas are hunting salmon here, and taking the occasional seal or sealion. They live in separate communities involving several families, and each social group is known as a pod. They focus on the mouth of the Tsitika River at the beautiful Robson Bight of Johnstone Strait, to take their toll of the Cohoe and Sockeye Salmon run.

Apart from the cormorants, the most obvious birds will be Common Guillemots (Murres in these parts) and Pigeon Guillemots – sea pigeons – easily identified by their white wing-patches. (Black Guillemots are as rare as Pigeon Guillemots are common.) Marbled Murrelets will be fairly common and mostly seen on the water.

Phalaropes

Red
Red-necked
Wilson's

Phalaropes are the only waders (shorebirds) which settle freely on the surface of the sea. And, unlike other waders, two of them spend all their time at sea outside the three-month breeding season (Wilson's Phalarope is very much more of an inland bird throughout the year, breeding by freshwater ponds of central North America). They are dainty birds, 6– 9in (7–23cm) in length (Wilson's is the largest). The straight needle-like bill is joined to a small head and a long neck. The sandpiper-like body is thickly plumaged so that the bird floats high like a cork, on a cushion of air. The legs are placed amidships, oval in section so that they offer least resistance in swimming, the toes have coot-like lobed webs, compressed and folding flat on the forward stroke.

In the breeding quarters they frequent shallow water where they up-end like ducks or spin in circles, stirring the bottom and encouraging small stuff to the surface to be picked off. Mosquito larvae and insects are prime prey. The centrally placed legs are

You may not be lucky enough to see the dorsal 'sail' of an Orca, sitting atop an animal which weighs up to 7 tonnes and reaching as much as 30ft (9m) in length. But you will certainly see what seems to be a miniature version. Dall's Porpoise, which, complete with oval and white blaze behind the eye, is an enthusiastic bow-wave rider. And you will certainly see enough Bald Eagles to satisfy the most avid raptor-ticker. But you need to get your eye in to catch them in the treetops as you pass.

The shores here are densely wooded, rising steeply to the bare peaks of the mountain range. It is classic temperate rain forest, wet, and with a mossy carpet. The dominant species are the giant Sitka Spruce and Western Hemlock, with Cottonwood and wild Crabapple along the freshwater banks. And while Sitka Spruce may not be a European favourite because of the forester's tendency to plant the trees in a regimented single-age monoculture, here in the north-west Pacific it is at home. In its natural element it offers a superb panorama and a home for a healthy population of Red Squirrels. The Hemlock shows as a bushier tree, darker

Overleaf:
Glacier Bay is a place of exceptional scenic beauty, to say nothing of the whales and Grizzly Bears, Tufted Puffins and Marbled Murrelets
TONY SOPER

unusual in sea-going birds but offer a clear advantage in swimming tight circles. At sea huge numbers feed on plankton in slicks or in convergence zones where offshore winds whip up the surface. They may cadge a lift on a whale's back, taking lice as they do so.

The Red and Red-necked Phalaropes breed in high northern latitudes, arriving at the freshwater ponds and rivers of the arctic and subarctic tundra in late May and early June. Astonishingly, they are examples of rôle-reversal from the sexual norm. The female is the larger and more brightly coloured, and it is she who chooses the nest-site and takes the lead in courtship activities. She lays the eggs and then leaves the male, who is suitably drably coloured

for the job, both to incubate and care for the young. Four eggs is usual, the chicks leave the nest after hatching and soon fend for themselves. If food is plentiful, the female may provide two males with clutches. Either way, she has departed for the coast before the chicks hatch (thereby making more food available for those remaining). The males follow first, then the juveniles, joining the females to moult in coastal waters before the long migration south to the winter quarters out at sea, where they spend the greater part of the year. In winter plumage the sexes are similar, all are drab. Phalaropes have a curiously weak flight, they are so light and airy they are often 'wrecked' ashore in large numbers in gales.

green, beside the dominant spruce. The joy of the spruce forest is to be able to see a spread of age groups occuring naturally with both young trees and over-the-hill specimens properly intermixed, as Nature meant them to be. The not infrequent bare patches are the end-product of infestation by an epidemic of spruce-bark beetles. The shoreline is littered with stranded logs

Auks

Little Auk	Ancient Murrelet
Razorbill	Crested Murrelet
Brunnich's Guillemot	Cassin's Auklet
Guillemot	Parakeet Auklet
Black Guillemot	Crested Auklet
Pigeon Guillemot	Least Auklet
Spectacled Guillemot	Whiskered Auklet
Marbled Murrelet	Rhinoceros Auklet
Kittlitz's Murrelet	Atlantic Puffin
Xantus's Murrelet	Horned Puffin
Craveri's Murrelet	Tufted Puffin

The name is said to come from the old Norse *alka,* meaning 'neck' (from the Razorbill's habit of stretching its neck when it returns to the nest ledge). There are twenty-two species in the family, which includes the guillemots (murres), murrelets, auklets and puffins. But the most famous member is extinct. The Great Auk of the North Atlantic was much bigger than its living relatives, but it was flightless, a condition which served it perfectly for its way of life but exposed it cruelly to the dep-

redations of sealers and fishermen who collected it for food or bait until it neared extinction in the early nineteenth century. By then its very rarity caused it to be hunted with ever greater zeal for 'academic' collections till the last survivor was killed in 1844, to join the Dodo as a pathetic memory.

The living auks are found almost entirely in the colder waters of the Northern Hemisphere (they are replaced in the Southern Hemisphere by the penguins and diving-petrels to which they are not related). They originate from and are most numerous in the North Pacific but are well represented in the North Atlantic and the Arctic Ocean. Medium-sized birds, they are mostly dark above and white below. They have dense waterproof plumage, often with brightly coloured bills and face parts, with plumed ornaments about the head. The heads are large, bills long and slender to short and blunt; legs placed well aft on a chunky body, short tail. They are divers and swimmers, using their small narrow wings to whirr in the air and to 'fly' underwater, something of a compromise. They don't fly as well as gulls or dive as well as penguins. The sexes are similar, to our eyes at least. Their flight is direct, somewhat desperate and a bit feeble; on the whole they prefer to move about by swimming.

bleached white by prolonged exposure to the sun.

Counting Bald Eagles as you traverse the Grenville Channel is a popular sport. Twelve is my personal best; you may do better but it won't be easy! The adults are easiest to spot because of the conspicuous white head, in sharp contrast to the black body. You can expect to see eagles every day. Sometimes the passage of the

Overleaf:
Black-legged Kittiwakes crowd the ledges on cliffs next to the tidewater glaciers. When the glaciers calve, the kittiwakes fly in to feast on the disturbed plankton
TONY SOPER

The larger *alcids,* like the puffins, feed on fish; small ones, like the auklets, on plankton. Some breed sociably, in huge colonies of many thousands, some in scattered groups, some solo. And like their southern counterparts they stand upright, a stance which we find endearing. They nest in a variety of situations, high up on mountainous scree slopes inland, on precipitous sea-cliffs or grassy cliff-top slopes in burrows, some in tree holes and some on tree branches. Some even patronise artificial nestboxes. Most make no formal nest but drop their egg or eggs on the bare rock or onto the soil. Puffins import some grass and feathers to improve their underground burrows.

Auks employ an unusual variety of breeding strategems within the family. In colonial species the chicks leave the nest-place synchronously, before they are able to fly, and are assiduously attended by the parents at sea. In the case of puffins, the chick is totally dependent on the parents which feed it in the underground burrow until it is larger than they are. They then abandon it to find its own way out into the open and to the sea when hunger forces the issue. But others of the family leave the nest a couple of days after hatching to go to sea with the parents. Murrelets are found only in the Pacific area, some in trees, some on the ground.

One of the remaining ornithological mysteries is provided by the Marbled Murrelet. Although a common bird, seen in hundreds of thousands in Alaskan waters, an everyday 'tick', its breeding arrangements are still much of a puzzle. Only a handful of 'nests' have ever been found, some on the ground and some on the mossy branches of trees, but the subarctic spruce and Western Hemlock forests of British Columbia and Alaska must hold the key to the mystery. What evidence there is suggests that mature trees are the preferred nest sites and of course these are the ones most at danger from logging operations.

Auks winter at sea in small or large flocks, normally not too far from the coast. At this time they lose the gaudy bill sheaths and moult through a flightless period. At sea they float high like gulls, but are more squat in shape. It has to be said that they are not easy to spot, though they are among the commonest birds in the Northern Hemisphere. There are literally millions of pairs of puffins and guillemots and other auks. But they seem to be in decline as a result of several factors which include oil and chemical pollution, disturbance and the increase in fishing activities by the primary competitor, man, which affects the abundance of prey species as well as trapping large numbers of birds in fishing- nets.

Tufted Puffins, above, *are common in the Alaskan fjords; Horned Puffins,* below, *less so*

ship disturbs them and they fly off, showing their white tails, well before the vessel comes alongside. Some fly past close to the ship and are easy to spot. But mostly they are sitting tight and you need to look carefully. Check the spruces or Cottonwoods closest to the shore. The birds tend to perch at the very tops of the trees at the edge of the beach or low cliff. Scan at treetop height for a white spot but remember the young birds are all dark.

The Bald Eagles are completely protected nowadays. When their nests are found they are tagged with a numbered yellow plate and logging is not permitted within 300ft (90m) of the tree. As a result the species, which is either rare or uncommon in the rest of its range, is abundant in the British Columbia and Alaskan panhandle region. The best estimate is something like 2,600 breeding pairs. Carrion feeders, mainly, they take freshly dead or dying fish which make up three-quarters of their diet in this region.

Once across the border, the first US town is Ketchikan, Alaska. And if you have time, take the harbour cruise, for at Ward Cove there is an impressive pulp mill with an equally impressive concentration of Bald Eagles, including waterside nests which will have eaglets in them. Ketchikan has a good museum and a fish hatchery which is open to view, but it is also the centre for a visit to Misty Fjords National Monument, a vast wilderness of weathered granite, hanging valleys and waterfalls of a classic temperate rain forest. There are Brown and Black Bears, Moose, Marten, Wolves, Wolverines and Mountain Goats. But sadly you'll see little of them from the sea.

Dall's Porpoise will guide you along the channels, though, and there is always the slight chance of a Grizzly Bear. In fact the population of bears is very high here, and the coastal grizzlies are the biggest specimens because of the plentiful salmon. A mature male will generally attain 900 pounds (400kg), but on the coast the beast may reach a massive 1,400 pounds (635kg). (If you meet one, incidentally, don't run away. It will usually move off. But if it does decide to attack, lie down and play dead. This way you're less likely to *become* dead, so they say.)

Up to three hundred Humpback Whales summer around Frederick Sound, at the southern end of Admiralty Island, and they tend to congregate for feeding on the rich krill near the Five Fingers

Light. If you are lucky you will see the great whales leap explosively from the sea, to slam their jaws shut and expel a giant spout of hundreds of gallons of seawater through the curtains of baleen, trapping the shrimp catch inside. This is the climax to behaviour known as bubble-net feeding, where a group of whales spiral down to the depths, blowing a screen of bubbles to enclose a mass of krill, then swim up inside the curtain with open mouths engulfing vast quantities of the shrimps.

South-east Alaska – the 'panhandle' region – has a population of about 50,000 people. There are some thousand islands, relatively few of them inhabited. (On Admiralty Island there are more bears than people and twice as many eagles' nests as there are houses.) The whole region is heavily dependent on ships and aircraft for supplies and communication. Juneau, the State capital, has no road connecting it with the world outside. But what it has got is the most northerly hummingbirds in the Americas, something that comes as a surprise to most of us! The Rufous Hummingbird winters in Central America, but migrates up the coast to Alaska to feed on the nectar of the Salmon Berry and to breed. Anna's Hummingbird also reaches up into Alaska, but is only sustained there by artificial feeding. The Rufous Hummingbird is an honest breeding bird, not much bigger than a moth and less than 4in (10cm) overall, While lying alongside the berth in Juneau, one came and perched briefly on the rail. Several times I have seen these bee-like birds from a ship well offshore, they buzz past full of confidence.

Juneau has herds of Moose in the river valleys, but they are not easy to see. Moose spend a great deal of time up to their knees in swampy ponds, munching willow twigs and grass. You may see them grazing on the large sandy flats at the entrance to the Katzehin River in Chilkoot Inlet on your way to Skagway or Haines. Haines offers excellent birding but it is at its best, for the waterfowl and shorebirds, in late April and early June. Trumpeter Swans breed here, also Harlequin Ducks, Scoters and Canvasbacks.

After retracing the Chilkoot Inlet from Skagway or Haines, the ship now turns north again and heads up to Icy Strait and the entrance to the sensational Glacier Bay. Off Point Adolphus there is a concentration of Humpback and Minke Whales. There is a better chance of seeing pods of Orcas here than almost anywhere

Harbour
Mew Gulls
Glaucous-winged Gulls
Bonaparte's Gulls
Great Blue Heron
Belted Kingfisher
Northwestern Crow
Bald Eagle
American Robin

Mendenhall Glacier
Rufous Hummingbird
Anna's Hummingbird
Yellow Warbler

Auke Lake
Chestnut-backed Chickadee

Gold Creek
Tree Swallow
Varied Thrush
Winter Wren
Harlequin Duck
American Dipper

Juneau, Alaska.
6 July 1988

Anna's Hummingbird is sustained by backyard feeders in penetrating north to Alaska, but it doesn't breed there

Bald Eagles are at home soaring in the icy wilderness of coastal Alaska
ANDY LOVELL

Northwestern Crow
Violet-green Swallow
Sharp-shinned Hawk
Pine Siskin
Bald Eagle
Belted Kingfisher
Song Sparrow
Raven
American Robin
Barn Swallow
Mew Gull
Hermit Thrush
Pigeon Guillemot
Greater Yellowlegs
Western Sandpiper
Moose
Mountain Goat
Trumpeter Swan
Red-necked Phalarope
Marbled Murrelet
Common Murre
White-winged Scoter
Red-breasted Merganser
Sabine's Gull
Glaucous-winged Gull

Skagway and Haines, Alaska.
7 July 1988

else in south-east Alaska, so watch for the huge dorsal fin, up to 6ft (1.8m) long in the male. The Humpbacks will be feeding. Lively, noisy and pleasantly ugly, warts, bumps and barnacle encrusted, they will be herding the abundant krill. Sooty Shearwaters may congregate at the scene to feed on the krill and plankton spilling from the whales' mouths or merely brought up by the turbulence. For a shearwater, whether the turbulence is the result of a collision of tidal streams or whale activity is of little consequence; their interest is in the available food.

Glacier Bay is one of the natural wonders of the world; a place of truly exceptional beauty. Giant tidewater glaciers, floating islands of ice and translucent blue-green water, rich with plankton. Nothing you read about it, in spite of all the superlatives and honest enthusiasm, prepares you for the immensity of the experience. Here the glaciers are receding – two hundred years ago Glacier Bay was just a dent in the shoreline, and as the ice recedes plants get a toe-hold. As the ship steams slowly up the bay you effectively step back in vegetational time. The dominant Sitka Spruce is preceded by Cottonwoods and Alders, then scrubby Dwarf Willow and mosses, then the ice-scraped barren rock and the flowing glaciers themselves. In Glacier Bay there are sixteen active glaciers, a live show of geological forces in action. Watch out on the scrubby slopes for bears and Moose, but they take some seeing. White and shaggy Mountain Goats may be high on the rocky slopes in the most inaccessible places.

At the tide-face of the glaciers, the sea is endlessly undermining the ice-cliffs. Every few minutes there is a thunderous crack as the calving ice parts. There is a mighty splash and a wave ripples out. And the Black-legged Kittiwakes scream in to pick up stunned shrimps from the surface water. The sea is littered with miniature icebergs – bergy bits – topped by Glaucous-winged Gulls. And believe it or not, there is an Ice Worm, some 3/4in (2cm) long and related to the garden earthworm, which lives in the glacier ice. It feeds on the red surface algae, migrating down into an ice hole if the sun gets too warm, for it prefers to tolerate temperatures just above freezing.

Harbour Seals bask on the bergy bits, along with the gulls. In the waters of the bay there are many Tufted and a few Horned Puffins, a few Kittlitz and many Marbled Murrelets. The murrelets are

Humpback Whales
Glaucous-winged Gull
Mew Gull
Black-legged Kittiwake
Kittlitz's Murrelet
Tufted Puffin
Double-crested Cormorant
Harbour Seal
Arctic Tern
Bald Eagles (on bergy bits)
Surf Scoter
Common Merganser
Black Bears, 2
White-winged Scoter
Red-necked Phalarope
Pelagic Cormorant
Sabine's Gull
Common Murre
Minke Whales
Horned Puffin
Dall's Porpoise
Jaeger sp.
Sooty Shearwaters

Icy Strait and Glacier Bay, Alaska.
8 July 1988

curious creatures. Marbled Murrelets breed all the way from Alaska down to California, presumably nesting off the ground on the branches of Larch or Hemlock, or Redwoods further south. The Kittlitz is a most mysterious bird about whose nesting habits practically nothing was known until recently. But apparently they nest, untypically for auks, in solitary splendour, laying on bare ground amongst snow-patches above the tree line. Most auks are conspicuously marked, but in breeding plumage Kittlitz is well camouflaged to cope with its exposed position.

At what passes for night-time in these latitudes look out for Fork-tailed Storm-Petrels. The Alaskan population is estimated at five million breeding pairs. With their swift darting and erratic flight, they seem drawn to ships' lights and are fairly common even close to the coast, though they are primarily offshore birds. Glaucous-winged Gulls are with you all the time but not Glaucous, which are very rare in the Gulf of Alaska. But you have a strong chance of seeing the truly pelagic Sabine's Gull. Arctic and Pomarine Skuas are likely. Arctic Terns may be seen riding on ice-floes or driftwood. Even Bald Eagles perch on the bergy bits of ice.

If you penetrate further north to Columbia Glacier then the same bird list is likely to result, but there will be many Harbour Seals and, a great pleasure, Sea Otters. The otters will be reclining on their backs in the approved style or, sometimes, up on the ice of the bergy bits.

Sea Otters are becoming more common in south-east Alaska, the result of effective protection through the years. Especially on the wild Pacific coast, in the outer islands, they are increasing mightily. If you are lucky enough to call at Sitka, make every effort to take a small-boat trip to St Lazaria Island, the most important seabird rookery in the panhandle, and with luck you will have close-up views of sea-going otters. Over the past few years they have been carefully re-introduced to several kelp bays north of Sitka, and it looks as if they are taking full advantage of the habitat which suits them. Steller's Sealions are resident here too.

There are also seabirds here, thousands of them. Black Oyster-catchers, Common Guillemots, Marbled, Kittlitz's and Ancient Murrelet, Cassin's and Rhinoceros Auklet, Tufted Puffins. All in all, a trip through the Inside Passage of British Columbia and Alaska is a birder's pilgrimage to Mecca.

Harbour Seals, 200
Bald Eagle on an ice-floe
American Oystercatcher
Mew Gulls
Glaucous-winged Gulls
Black-legged Kittiwakes
Salmon jumping
Arctic Terns, 2 (riding a stick)
Sea Otter (with young on chest)
Marbled Murrelet
Pelagic Cormorant
Common Loons, 3
Sea Otters (50+ on bergy bits)
Dall's Porpoises

College Fjord, Alaska.
9 July 1988

SOUTH ATLANTIC

Off the northern coast of Brazil, Masked and Red-footed Boobies are likely to join the ship, the latter especially addicted to perching in the rigging. Since they exist in a most bewildering range of brown, grey and white plumages, the red feet are a gesture of kindness in identification. Perching in the rigging comes easily to them as they are the only tree-nesting boobies and know all about swaying in the wind. They are also to a certain extent nocturnal, and turn this to advantage when perching on forestay, foredeck davit or forecastle head. Like the other boobies they take flying fish both in the sea and in flight. But at night, (especially in the equatorial Atlantic part of their range),Flying Squid come to the surface. A passing ship will disturb these cephalopods – the only flying snails – and their escape reaction matches their behaviour when chased by a tunny or a dolphin fish. Jet-powered, they back away from perceived trouble by jumping clear of the water, stretching their lateral fins to glide as much as 150ft (45m), vulnerable to chase by the Red-footed Boobies.

There is a great deal of seabird activity associated with the rich fishing-ground of the continental shelf off northern Brazil. In spring and autumn there will be Wilson's Storm-Petrels and Sooty Shearwaters on passage to and from the Caribbean and North Atlantic. From October, Great Shearwaters will be working their way south from the western North Atlantic on the way to breeding-places on remote South Atlantic islands. Cory's Shearwaters, too,

176

'winter' in these waters, from Ascension down to the Falklands. The continental shelf provides plenty of fish for these passing birds, but so also do the disturbed areas around islands such as Ascension, wherever a deep-water current meets an obstruction.

Fish-shoals around Ascension will be a magnet for Cory's and Great Shearwaters, but also for the large numbers of Sooty Terns which, as 'wideawakes', breed at the Wideawake Fairs on this remote island. Large numbers there may be, (on the one occasion

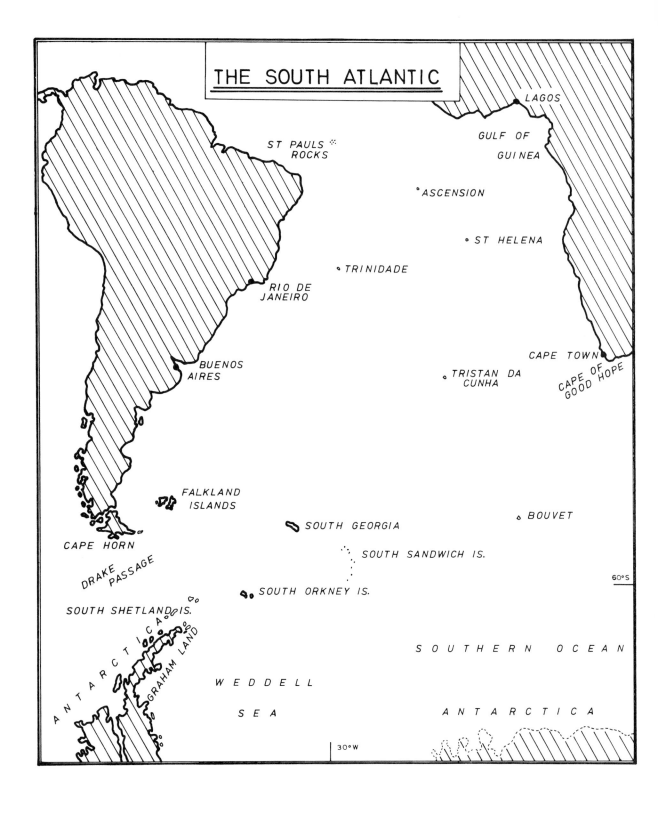

when I had the privilege of visiting the fair site there wasn't a bird to be seen!) but they are nothing to the multitudes there used to be. For Ascension is an only too typical example of a remote island whose immense breeding populations of seabirds have been reduced to a pathetic remnant because of the devastation caused by the introduction of exotic predators by man. Nowadays the main colonies of bosun birds (tropicbirds) and Ascension Frigatebirds are confined to offshore islets, but the Sooty Terns still crowd to the Wideawake Fair. Since there are no trees or bushes any more there are no breeding Red-footed Boobies.

Brazilian harbours offer Kelp, Brown-hooded and Grey-headed Gulls, and from Rio south the sea-swallows will be mostly South American Terns. In the cold temperate waters pelagic seabirds

Black Vulture
Peregrine
Peruvian Pelican
Kelp Gull
Band-tailed Gull
Elegant Tern
Franklin's Gull
Laughing Gull
Sandwich Tern
Royal Tern
South American Tern

*Callao Harbour,
Lima, Peru.
25 Jan 1986,
Bernard Watts*

Giant Petrels are small-albatross-sized scavengers, rejoicing in the whaler's name of Stinker. They range the southern ocean, riding the gales of the 'roaring forties' right round the Antarctic continent

Below;
Wandering Albatross, in intermediate plumage between the all-chocolate juvenile and the snowy-white adult
RNBWS

At length did cross an albatross,
Thorough the fog it came;...
It ate the food it ne'er had eat.
And round and round it flew

THE ANCIENT MARINER
COLERIDGE

rapidly become more numerous. Prions and petrels begin to follow the ship. The prions – whalebirds – have a distinctive wide-open 'W' mark on their wings. The commonest ship-following petrel in these parts is the piebald Cape Petrel, a strikingly patterned bird of the southern oceans, breeding on Antarctica and subantarctic islands. It is an enthusiastic ship-fancier, following in flocks for galley waste or offal, and becoming ever-more common the further south you go.

Along with the petrels and prions come the first of the South Atlantic albatrosses. From about 25⁰ South the first to appear will most likely be the Yellow-nosed, which has more inclination for warm water; but further south the greatest in size and the most enthusiastic ship-follower appears – the mighty Wandering Albatross with its 12ft (3.5m) span.

Westerly winds predominate once you approach the roaring forties, and nine species of albatross range the southern oceans, gliding on the eternal winds and exploring the food-rich cold currents which reach up from the Antarctic ice. They tend to drift with the wind, revolving round the Antarctic continent. The wanderers are in reality mostly immature birds in their roving stage. Lance Tickell found that many of the birds he ringed at the nest in South Georgia travelled as far as the coasts of Australia. And in the southern winter many of them found their way well up the coast of South Africa.

At sea, and beyond the Patagonian shelf-edge, there are more Royal Albatrosses than wanderers, but because the Royals are more shy of ships it is more likely the Wandering Albatross that you will see. The Royal Albatross breeds far away in New Zealand,

Black-browed Albatrosses are probably the most widespread and common of all the family. Hundreds of thousands breed in the Falkland Islands. The black eye-streak gives them their name and the scowling expression
RNBWS

but, like the others, is free of the circumpolar winds. In the latter part of the year Cape Petrels and Antarctic Fulmars will be moving south to breeding areas. At sea, on passage for the Falkland Islands, there will be Giant Petrels, birds which win no popularity contests with seafarers, burdened with the common name of stinker because of their lack of table manners in pursuit of garbage or offal of all kinds. Antarctic Fulmars, Kerguelen, White-chinned and Grey Petrels are widespread offshore, Great Shearwaters and South American terns, too.

By penguin standards immature birds travel great distances but since they have to swim, the miles are measured in hundreds at most. In fact you will be lucky to spot penguins at sea, but Magel-

Peruvian Pelican
Peruvian Booby
Franklin's Gull
Kelp Gull
Olivaceous Cormorant
Elegant Tern
Laughing Gull

Valparaiso Harbour, Chile.
29 Jan 1986
Bernard Watts

Albatrosses

Wandering	Buller's
Royal	White-capped
Waved	Yellow-nosed
Short-tailed	Grey-headed
Black-footed	Amsterdam
Laysan	Sooty
Black-browed	Light-mantled

The name is an English sailors' corruption of the Portuguese 'alcatraz' for pelican, a bird which early explorers would have known from the Mediterranean. In practical terms, the fourteen species are crudely divided into 'great albatrosses', the Wandering and Royal; and the 'small albatrosses', collectively better known to seafarers as mollymawks, from the Dutch 'mal', foolish, and 'mok', gull. Another term for them is 'gooney', from the English dialect word for simpleton. These pejorative and richly undeserved epithets were the result partly of seeing albatrosses ashore, out of their element, appearing clumsy, and partly because of their endearing but ill-advised innocence in standing quietly while being bludgeoned by a club and picked up for the pot.

Albatrosses have stout bodies with large heads on long necks, short tails mostly and strikingly long and narrow wings (to nearly 12ft (3.6m) in the Wanderer). They have short legs, placed well back but the most eye-catching feature is the massive hooked bill, covered with a number of horny plates. Great albatrosses are mainly white, the twelve smaller ones have variable quantities of black on the back as well as on the wings. Most are inhabitants of the southern oceans, mainly between 30° and 60° South. But one is based on the equatorial Galapagos Islands, ranging the Humboldt area. Three are confined to the North Pacific, effectively isolated from their southern cousins by the windless region of the

lanics may be as much as 200 miles (320km) from land. In calm weather, they reveal themselves as they surface after diving. Gentoo and Rockhopper Penguins become more possible as you close to within 70 miles (110km) of the Falklands.

Black-browed Albatrosses, which have probably only been seen as wandering immatures, now appear as adults, even rafting offshore in some numbers. Turbulent offshore currents bring Lobster Krill to the surface inside the 200-mile (320km) exclusion zone of the Falklands. Where the foreign fleets congregate for fishing, watch for Grey-headed Albatrosses but Giant Petrels will be here in force as well. Dark, heavy birds which look superficially like young albatrosses but lack their grace, flying as stiff gliders

doldrums.

Albatrosses spend most of their lives in flight, gliding the waves and circling the major wind systems. They are highly accomplished dynamic soarers, seemingly motionless yet totally in control but they rely on a constant supply of wind and are highly inefficient in flapping flight. In the occasional calm they are forced to sit it out on the surface and wait.

Their food is mainly squid, taken when they settle on the water, when they float high with plenty of freeboard, wings usually raised to keep them dry. They will also examine floating weed in the hope of finding fish eggs and they will follow ships for galley waste.

They are slow to mature, mollymawks breeding in their sixth or seventh year, great albatrosses in their ninth. Giving evidence of their southern origins, even the North Pacific species breed at the time of the southern summer, October–April. They all breed colonially, on remote oceanic islands. Mating for life, they court with dances which may seem somewhat ungainly to us, bowing and scraping, bill rubbing and wing stretching. The nest is a scrape on the ground or a mud-mound lined with a few feathers or grasses. The single chick is fed by regurgitation of stomach oil. The process is long drawn out, from egg-laying to fledging takes nearly a year in the case of the great albatrosses, as a consequence they breed only in alternate years. But, all being well, they may live to be fifty years of age.

In the past they were much persecuted both for their meat and their plumage. Taken in significant numbers on hook and line by sailors who made pouches out of their webbed feet, feather rugs from their skins and pipe stems from their bones, they suffered most severely in the latter part of the nineteenth century when Japanese plume-hunters nearly exterminated the North Pacific populations. The feathers were processed and sold as 'swan's down' for mattresses. Under protection, they have increased.

with shorter wings. The stinkers are voracious scavengers – sea vultures. They specialise in offal, looking for dead or near-dead birds, seals and whale carcasses.

Approaching Port Stanley there will be South American and Antarctic Terns throughout the year. The gulls of the southern oceans are generally found close in to land and Stanley is no exception, though Kelp Gulls may be as much as 30 miles (50km) off. In the harbour there will be the delightful Dolphin Gulls and Flightless Steamer Ducks. In the hawse-holes of the abandoned sailing ship hulks Rock Shags make their nests and gaze upon a less-troubled world. And, for proof that Stanley has found itself dragged into a new age, there are organised rambles which, avoiding the minefields, take you to see penguins and the infamous Giant Petrels at the town dump.

Penguins are superb fliers, but in water rather then air. Rockhopper chasing an Ice Fish

Giant Petrels squabbling over food
ERIC & DAVID HOSKING

The main islands in the Falkland group are somewhat barren, though there are Upland Geese and caracaras. The sedimentary rocks are covered in peaty or marshy moorland and mainly grazed short by sheep. Unfortunately, introduced foxes, cats and rodents have devastated the mainland wildlife but outlying islets are still clothed in the splendidly tall tussock grass and abound with life from penguins to Kelp Geese, sheathbills and cormorants, gulls and sealions.

The southern entrance to the Falkland Sound, which divides the two main islands, East and West Falkland, is a prime area for seabird concentrations because of a fruitful meeting of winds and currents. There may be hundreds of Black-browed Albatrosses,

Penguins

Emperor
King
Adélie
Gentoo
Chinstrap
Fiordland Crested
Erect-crested
Rockhopper
Macaroni

Royal
Snares Island
Yellow-eyed
Little
Jackass
Peruvian
Magellanic
Galapagos

Highly adapted to underwater hunting, penguins are flightless in air. Their compact, streamlined bodies have a deep keel for a breastbone and massive paddle-muscles. Their legs are set well back on the body, giving them their rolling gait. They are highly sociable birds, both at sea and ashore, breeding in colonies which can involve millions of pairs. They are almost entirely restricted to the Southern Hemisphere; the invisible barrier of warm tropical water denies them access to the northern fishing waters. Those few which breed in tropical or temperate habitats do so underground to avoid the sun.

Rockhopper Penguin

Length 25in (63cm). Distinguished from other crested penguins by smaller size, red eyes and drooping crest. Much confused with Macaroni Penguin.

Circumpolar in mainly temperate sub antarctic: Macquarie, Auckland, Campbell, Antipodes, Kerguelen, Tristan da Cunha, Falklands, Tierra del Fuego, etc.

Most aggressive of the penguins; will attack intruders with gusto, even jumping up to fasten to a sleeve and hold on furiously. Rookeries formed on rocky coastline. Two bluish-white eggs laid in a nest of pebbles or grass (according to terrain). Nests often in caves or crevices, or on open terraces. Breeding schedule varies according to location. Progresses in a series of bounds.

Predators: on land, skuas and gulls. At sea, Leopard Seals. Much exploited by man for eggs and oil in the past.

King Penguin

Length 3ft (90cm). Weighs 30 to 40lb (14 to 18kg). Similar in appearance to Emperor Penguin, but differs in size and in having brighter yellow colouration.

Breeds in the Antarctic and sub antarctic islands (being replaced on polar coasts by the Emperor), on Prince Edward, Crozet, Kerguelen, Heard, Macquarie, South Georgia, South Sandwich and Staten Islands. Wanders north to Tierra del Fuego and the Falklands. Rookeries are always on low, bare ground, where the birds incubate the single egg in a fashion similar to that of the Emperor. Incubation period is about fifty-four days, both parents sharing. Kings are more or less sedentary; their shore territory is never completely choked with ice, and their food, squid and sprats, is close at hand in the inshore kelp-beds.

At sea, the main predator is the Leopard Seal. On shore, man has wrought enormous damage over the years, many hundreds of thousands of birds having been taken for their plumage and their blubber, with the result that the range of the species is much reduced, although its numbers are now increasing.

Adélie Penguin

Length about 30in (75cm). The most familiar of all penguins, the smart little man in evening dress. Weight about 9–14lb (4–6kg) dropping to 6–10lb (3–5kg) after the breeding season.

Antarctic and circumpolar. Most abundant and widely distributed of all Antarctic penguins. Vagrant to South Georgia, Heard Island and Macquarie Island. Does not breed north of the South Sandwich and Bouvet Islands.

Adélies return to the rookery during October,when the sea is still frozen and they may have to cross as much as 60miles (100km) of ice. They nest at the foot of gentle ice-cliff slopes. Experienced breeders return to the same nest site and construct a nest pile of small stones (no other material is available) on open ground. Two eggs (sometimes only one but never three), incubated at first by male while female goes off to feed at sea (mainly on shrimps), returning to relieve her mate two weeks later. Subsequently they take turns in departing for feeding expeditions. Incubation period is about thirty-six days. Both parents feed the young, which after four weeks congregate in crèches of as many as a hundred or more chicks. Returning parents recognise and feed their own chicks in the group. Juveniles moult, then go to sea in February. Walking speed about 3 miles (5km) an hour, but Adèlies can run or toboggan much faster, outdistancing a sprinting man.

Predators at the rookery are sheathbills and Antarctic Skuas, but the weather is a more important enemy, many birds being buried at their nests by snow blizzards. At sea the main predator is the Leopard Seal.

Emperor Penguin

Length 4ft (120cm). Long, rather slender and decurved bill, patches of orange-yellow at sides of neck. Weighs from 50 to 100lb 23 to 45kg). One of the world's largest and heaviest seabirds. Although substantially heavier than the King Penguin, it has relatively smaller wings, feet and bill, factors favouring heat retention.

Breeds only on the continent of Antarctica, assembling on the sea-ice below ice-cliffs. The most truly Antarctic of all birds. No nest. After the egg is laid, soon after the sea ice forms in autumn, the male takes charge of it, carrying it on top of the feet, warmed by a fold of skin on his belly. While the male fasts, the female travels, perhaps many miles, across the sea-ice in order to reach open water and feed. Towards the end of the sixty-day incubation period she returns to relieve the male and feed the chick. The males then disperse after the long fast. The young are reared during the winter months achieving independence during the short summer season when food is abundant. In October and November, at the beginning of the Antarctic summer, they begin an extraordinary migration, congregating in groups at the edge of the sea-ice, waiting for the ice to break and provide ice-floe rafts on which they drift northward. The survival of the juvenile depends on their ice-floe lasting long enough to allow them to complete their moult before they have to enter the water.

Emperors normally walk bolt upright, but if alarmed they drop down and 'toboggan', using wings and legs to propel themselves. Main predators are Sea Leopards and Orcas.

Previous page:
*Gentoos are the largest
common penguin in the
Falklands. From their
landing beaches they may
have to walk as much as 3
miles (4.8km) to their
breeding-grounds, but these
usually have a sea view*
ERIC & DAVID HOSKING

*Breeding seabirds on the
Falkland Islands*

Gentoo Penguin
Macaroni Penguin
Rockhopper Penguin
Magellanic Penguin
Black-browed Albatross
Grey-headed Albatross
Giant Petrel
White-chinned Petrel
Thin-billed Prion
Fairy Prion
Great Shearwater
Sooty Shearwater
Wilson's Storm-Petrel
Grey-backed Storm-Petrel
Common Diving-Petrel
Rock Shag
Imperial Shag
Kelp Gull
Dolphin Gull
Brown-hooded Gull
South American Tern

tens of Royal and the odd White-capped Albatross. In Fox Bay a flock of 80,000 Sooty Shearwaters was seen compacted together on a square mile of surface. They breed on Kidney Island, but the large numbers come from southern South America.

West Point Island is privately owned, but with a tactful approach by prior contact you may be able to visit the Black-browed Albatross Colony, which is cheek by jowl with vast numbers of Rockhopper Penguins. On Steeple Jason Island there are said to be literally millions of albatrosses and penguins, plus petrel colonies and breeding Striated Caracaras. Some Rockhopper colonies are reliably estimated to contain two and a half million breeding pairs. In all, some fifty species of birds breed on these windy and seemingly barren islands.

Leaving the Falklands, on passage to South Georgia, you enter the Scotia Sea and the Antarctic, the richest area of plant plankton in the world's seas. In the short Antarctic summer these plants feed krill in astronomical populations, estimated at 30,000 individual shrimps per cubic metre of surface water – a biomass which in turn supports life for the great whales which summer here. The subpolar zones teem with invertebrate life, not in terms of species diversity but in sheer numbers of individuals. The situation here is the exact opposite of the tropics where pelagic areas have relatively few individuals from a wide variety of species. The great concentrations of polar marine organisms impart an intense greenish glow to the surface water, again a contrast to the deep sterile blue of much of the equatorial oceans.

The Arctic Terns which breed in high and subarctic northern latitudes in the northern summer are found here in these mirror-image high southern latitudes in the southern summer. Circling the south polar continent on the westerlies they see more daylight in their year than any other living creature – a life of perpetual summer. It is while they are in the Antarctic that they moult, before the return flight to the Arctic to breed.

King Penguins may be seen in the inshore waters off South Georgia, where they occupy large colonies. Various albatrosses breed here, with White-chinned Petrel and the diminutive Snow Petrel, as white as the ice-floes and bergy bits it haunts. Imperial Shags and Yellow-billed Pintail can be seen in Leith harbour, along with Giant Petrels and American Sheathbills. The harbour is the site of an old whaling station; there is another at Grytviken in Cumberland Bay, which again is well supplied with the many birds which are content to live in close proximity to men. In summer the beach is used by breeding Elephant Seals. If your vessel lies at anchor in these sheltered bays on an overcast night then petrels, prions, storm- and diving-petrels may come to the lights.

Five thousand pairs of Wandering Albatrosses breed on South Georgia, a quarter of Lance Tickell's estimate of the world breeding population – the total world population may be sixty thousand individuals, but mind-boggling numbers of breeding birds are typical of the Antarctic. On the South Sandwich Islands, the next group on from South Georgia, there is a Chinstrap Penguin colony estimated as home for ten million pairs. And some of the islets in the volcanic group are probably unexplored. Captain James Cook called it '. . . the most horrible coast in the world', but of course he wasn't a bird.

At sea off the South Shetland Islands, en route to Graham Land on the Antarctic peninsula, there may be large rafts of Adélie Penguins. They have been seen in thousands, submerging in unison on the approach of a ship.

Leaving the islands, there are few breeding species on the shores of the Antarctic continent, but four of them are tube-noses: the Antarctic Fulmar; Giant Petrel; Snow Petrel and the indefatigable Wilson's Storm-Petrel, a diminutive creature which may actually stumble through the snow to reach its burrow. Half a dozen penguins breed on this icy and inhospitable continent, joined nowadays by an increasing number of scientists, exploiters and, occasionally, honest sightseers. And one of those polar penguins, the mighty Emperor, breeds nowhere else on the planet.

You will be lucky to see an Emperor, but set foot on Graham Land and you will be visited by an American Sheathbill; the bird will come and join you if you sit still long enough. The sheathbills are the Antarctic version of gulls or waders, pottering about the sealion or bird colonies or outside an expedition galley, tidying up any refuse. As general scavengers, they steal eggs or chicks and patrol the sealion beaches on the lookout for afterbirths. Dumpy, rather pigeon-like birds, they have stout blunt bills with a horny sheath. Tame and inquisitive, they often land on ships at sea and take advantage of soft-hearted seamen and their galley scraps.

Giant Petrel
White-chinned Petrel
Black-browed Albatross
Wilson's Storm-Petrel
Rock Shag
Kelp Gull
Antarctic Tern
Magellanic Penguin
Wandering Albatross

Straits of Magellan.
2 Feb 1986,
Bernard Watts

Two of them joined the research ship *John Biscoe* while she was at the South Orkneys, taking passage to Port Stanley, where they went ashore. When she sailed again, yet another sheathbill came aboard and stayed to Montevideo, roosting in a sheltered part of the deck but periodically taking a turn out to sea.

Another sheathbill found itself on a naval vessel not long after the Falklands war, and stayed aboard all the way home to Plymouth, on the wrong side of the world, to be welcomed as a hero and become a twitcher's nine-day wonder. But it is said that this bird was 'persuaded' to make the journey by Chinese crew members.

Perhaps the most astonishing and unlikely bird to join a ship in these fearsome latitudes is a Cattle Egret, yet in their dogged determination to colonise the world they have turned up on ships all over the place, right down to 61° South. Truly you need to keep a weather eye open as a sea-going birdwatcher.

Arctic Terns swoop on their surface prey from a low height and do not even get their feet wet

APPENDICES

FIRST AID

Birds are attracted to ships as by a magnet. Sometimes they come to grief by collision and sometimes they come aboard because they are exhausted. But before you rush to their assistance make sure, as best you can, that they actually need help. Remember that most often they are using the ship as a fishing look-out perch or because they simply want to rest. If this is the case they are best left alone and enjoyed from a respectful distance. They are certainly not asking for food or water.

Trouble very often strikes at night, when, for example, Sooty Terns and tropicbirds, less often petrels and storm-petrels, deliberately approach the ship searching for the plankton or squid thrown up by the action of the propellors or just disturbed by the passage of the vessel. Sometimes they are blinded or disoriented, crash and end up in the scuppers or some corner. If they are not injured they may still shuffle about with wings awry (for they can't walk at the best of times) but they cannot do vertical take-offs and are trapped.

You must judge whether the bird is full of vigour but 'lost', in which case all you need to do is pick it up and launch it over the side, giving it a bit of lift but not a baseball throw. Very often the bird seems dazed and in shock, in which case its main requirements are warmth (not heat), peace, quiet and the darkness of a cardboard box. Put a piece of towel or an old shirt in the bottom so that it doesn't roll about too much. Pierce plenty of ventilation holes and cover the top to provide darkness but air. Ninety-nine times out of a hundred the bird will not want food, and if it is a seabird it certainly will not drink. With luck, it will be better in the morning, signalling its desire for freedom by scratching about and flapping its wings when you disturb it. And if it is dead, at least you tried. Next time you will be better able to judge whether or not the kindest response to a victim is to kill it as humanely as possible.

Oiled birds present a very different problem. They, too may need a period of rest before the oil is cleaned off, in which case it is important to prevent the patient from preening (and ingesting the oil, with dire consequences). Bundle it into old towelling or feed it into a sock with the toe-end cut off, so that it is literally unable to preen.

If it seems necessary to feed it, it will almost certainly need force-feeding, for seabirds have no experience of canned sardines and simply don't recognise them as food. Straddle the bird, gently force its mandibles apart and introduce a morsel of suitable size. Fresh sprats or sand-eels are ideal, but sardine pieces (oily, not in tomato sauce), minced meat or chopped raw fish will serve. All being well, they soon get the message.

To clean the oil off, first immobilise the beak with a rubber band. Massage the plumage, *always* with the lay of the feathers, with weak detergent in warm water. When the oil is cleared, rinse the plumage. And this is the point where most oiled-bird cleaning goes wrong for it is vitally important to rinse every last vestige of detergent from the feathers. This means the bird must spend at least thirty minutes under a warm shower after the first 'heavy-duty' rinsing. Take off the rubber band, keep the bird warm until it is thoroughly dry and has had a serious preening session. And, provided it will feed, keep it for several days before release. Release them *into* the wind, (from a good height in the case of terns and tropicbirds) and from the after-part of the ship, so that there is no danger of it colliding again.

Landbirds must be fed and treated as you would any sick bird ashore. Seeds for the nut-cracker-billed, scrambled egg and worm/fly substitute for the thinner-softbills, raw meat and roughage (feathers or furry skin) for the hooked-beak raptors – all will welcome fresh water.

Birds with broken bones or internal injuries need professional attention. If it is not available you must seriously consider killing the bird as the kindest alternative to prolonged agony, though this is a most difficult decision to take.

WILDLIFE CRUISE OPERATORS

OCEAN-GOING
Canberra Cruises & Princess Voyages
77 New Oxford Street, London WC1A 1PP.
(Write to Tony Soper, Gerston Point,
Kingsbridge, Devon TQ7 3BA for details.)
Society Expeditions Inc
(in USA) 3131 Elliot Avenue, Suite 700, Seattle,
Washington 98121, USA.
(in UK) Twickers World 22 Church St,
Twickenham TW13NW.
Special Expeditions Inc (in USA)
720 Fifth Avenue, New York, NY 10018, USA.

CALIFORNIA AND ALASKA
Biological Journeys Inc
1876 Ocean Drive, McKileyville, CA 95521,
USA for Baja California (Mexico), San Francisco
Bay and Alaska.
Princess Voyages
(as above, check with Tony Soper) Alaska.
Shearwater Journeys
(408-425-8111) for pelagic birds in Monterey
Bay, California.
Chris' Fishing Trips
48 Fisherman's Wharf, Monterey CA 93940,
USA, for whale-watching, Dec–Feb and March–
April.

MEDITERRANEAN
Write to Trevor Gunton, RSPB, Sandy, Beds.
SG19 2DL, UK, for details of Nile,
Mediterranean and Danube cruises led by RSPB
staff with Swan Hellenic.

WESTERN APPROACHES
Peter Harrison organises trips to the 'Wilson's
Triangle'. Phone Carol Harrison for details
(0736) 871564.
Pelagic seawatch off Cape Clear, with Peter
Harrison,
Branta Holidays,
11 Uxbridge Street, London W8 7QT.

NORTH AND NORWEGIAN SEAS
Harwich to Esbjerg for shearwaters, skuas and
gulls. **Branta Holidays** (see address above).
Norwegian Fjords to North Cape and Spitz
bergen (Tony Soper, address as above).
Norwegian Fjords to the North Cape, with Peter
Harrison, **Branta Holidays** (see address above).

Information on additional guided wildlife trips,
whether one hour or three months, will be much
appreciated for use in a proposed *World Directory
of Wildlife Cruises.*
Please write to Tony Soper (see address above).

Opposite:

The observation decks of P&O's cruise-liner Royal Princess *are ideal for whale- and seabird-watching from Alaska to the Caribbean*
TONY SOPER

Blackpoll Warbler, enjoying convalescence in Captain Westwater's cabin aboard MV Irma M.
CAPTAIN R.L.WESTWATER, MN/RNBW

Black-and-white Warbler, on assisted passage, poses while its details are recorded on a report form for the Royal Naval Bird-watching Society
CAPTAIN R.L.WESTWATER, MN/RNBWS

RECOMMENDED FIELD GUIDES AND SEABIRD BOOKS

The pelagic birder's ditty-bag. . .should contain a pocket notebook and pencil, of course, as well as Autan mosquito repellent! A pair of marine binoculars, 7 x 50, is the classic choice, but I have found the Zeiss 10 x 40 BGAT as rewarding to handle at sea as on land. A telescope is occasionally practical, but only in sheltered waters and from a steady deck.

The most valuable books of all are Peter Harrison's *Seabirds: An Identification Guide* (Croom Helm) and its companion volume of photographs, *Seabirds of the World: A Photographic Guide* (Christopher Helm), but Captain G.S. Tuck's *Field Guide to the Seabirds of Britain and the World* still has great value as a pocket book though inevitably it suffers from the use of outdated English names and will be infinitely more useful when there is a revised edition. Gerald Tuck's *A Guide to Seabirds on the Ocean Routes* is also most useful, though again its English names need to be checked with caution.

For general introductions to birds at sea I would particularly recommend three books. . . Bryan Nelson's *Seabirds: Their Biology and Ecology* (Hamlyn), Lars Löfgren's *Ocean Birds* (Croom Helm) and R.M. Lockley's *Ocean Wanderers* (David & Charles). The latter is a sheer pleasure to read. John Gooders' *Finding Birds Around the World* (André Deutsch) is a useful guide for likely shore-trips, but I wish he would hurry up and double its length in a revised edition. Currently, the regional field guides which will most adequately complement Peter Harrison's sea-going volumes are . . .

NORTH AND WESTERN EUROPE
Bardarson, H. *Birds of Iceland* (Bardarson, 1986)
Cramp, S. *et al. The Seabirds of Britain and Ireland* (Collins, 1974)
Heinzel, H. *et al. The Birds of Britain and Europe* (Collins, 1984)

NORTH ATLANTIC
Bannerman, D.A. *Birds of the Atlantic Islands* (Oliver & Boyd, 1963)

CARIBBEAN AND CENTRAL AMERICA
Bond, James. *Birds of the West Indies* (Collins, 1985)
Brudenell-Bruce, P.G.C. *The Birds of New Providence and the Bahama Islands* (Collins, 1975)
Ridley, R.S. *A Guide to the Birds of Panama* (Princeton U P, 1981)
Schauensee, R.M. de, *Birds of Venezuela* (Princeton UP, 1978)
Voous, Dr K.H. *Birds of the Netherlands Antilles* (De Walburg Pers, 1983)

CANADA AND THE UNITED STATES
Armstrong, Robert. *Guide to the Birds of Alaska* (Alaska Northwest Publishing, 1986)
Lane, James A. *A Birder's Guide to Florida* (L & P Press, 1984, PO Box 21604 Denver, Colorada 80221)
National Geographic Society. *A Field Guide to the Birds of North America* (NGS/David & Charles, 1987)
Scanlan-Rohrer, Anne. *San Francisco Peninsula Birdwatching* (Sequoia Audubon Society, 1985)

THE PACIFIC ISLANDS
Harris, M. *A Field Guide to the Birds of Galapagos* (Collins, 1974)
Pratt, H.D. *et al. A field Guide to the Birds of Hawaii and the Tropical Pacific* (Princeton U P, 1987)
Watling, Dick. *Birds of Fiji, Tonga and Samoa* (Millwood Press, NZ, 1982)

NEW ZEALAND
Falla, R. A. *et al. A Field Guide to the Birds of New Zealand* (Collins, 1966)

AUSTRALASIA

Bechler, B. *et al. Birds of New Guinea* (Princeton U P, 1986)

Pizzey, Graham. *.A field Guide to the Birds of Australia* (Collins, 1986)

Simpson, K. and Day, N. *Birds of Australia* (Christopher Helm, 1987)

THE FAR EAST

Brazil, Mark. *A Birdwatcher's Guide to Japan* (Harper & Row, 1988)

King, Ben *et al. A Field Guide to the Birds of SE Asia* (Collins, 1975)

Massey, J. *et al. A Field Guide to the Birds of Japan* (Wild Bird Society of Japan)

Schauensee R. M. de. *The Birds of China* (OUP, 1989)

Viney, C. & Phillips, K. *The Birds of Hong Kong* (Government Printer, Hong Kong, 1988)

INDIAN OCEAN

Ellis, R. *Guide to Mauritious* (Bradt, 1989)

Penny, Malcolm. *The Birds of Seychelles* (Collins, 1974)

Shepherd, M. *Let's Look at Sri Lanka* (Ornitholidays, 1978)

Williams, J. G. *A Field Guide to the Birds of The Indian Sub-continent* (Collins, 1976)

MEDITERRANEAN AND MIDDLE EAST

Bannerman, D. A. *Birds of Cyprus* (Oliver & Boyd)

Busby, J. *Birds of Mallorca* (Christopher Helm, 1988)

Flint, P. R. *The Birds of Cyprus* (British Ornithologists Union, 1983)

Hollom, P.A.D. *et al. Birds of the Middle East and North Africa* (T. & A. D. Poyser, 1988)

Goodman, S. M. (Ed) *The Birds of Egypt* (OUP, 1989)

Paz, Uzi. *The Birds of Israel* (Christopher Helm, 1987)

Watkinson, Eddie. *A Guide to Birwatching in Mallorca* (J. G. Sanders, St Anne, 1982)

THE SOUTHERN OCEAN

Moss, Sandford. *Natural History of the Antarctic Peninsula* (Princeton U P, 1989)

Murphy, R. C. *Oceanic Birds of South America* (Macmillan, 1936)

Woods, R.W. *Guide to Birds of the Falkland Islands* (Anthony Nelson, 1988)

WHALE-WATCHING

Leatherhead, S. and Reeves, R. P. *Whales and Dolphins* (Sierra Club, San Francisco, 1983)

Watson, Lyall. *Sea Guide to Whales of the World* (Hutchinson, 1981)

. . .and finally, don't forget to insure your camera and binoculars, and take photocopies of your policy information so that you can report losses without delay. Even faraway beaches have their share of those who try to spoil your day, don't let them get away with it!

The Natural History Book Service Ltd, 2 Wills Road, Totnes, Devon TQ9 5XN (0803 865913) is a useful book supplier if your local bookshop is unable to help. They produce a first-class bi-annual catalogue of new books. For scarce and second-hand books try Wheldon & Wesley, Lytton Lodge, Codicote, Hitchin, Herts SG4 8TE (0438 820370).

Steve Whitehouse, 5 Stanway Close, Blackpole, Worcester WR4 9XL, offers a unique service of birdwatching reports which list species and describe actual visits to locations all over the world. Write for catalogue.

SEABIRD ORGANISATIONS

IN THE UK . . .

The Royal Naval Birdwatching Society
(Hon Secretary: Col P.J.S. Smith RM, 19 Downlands Way, South Wonston, Winchester SO21 3HS). Established in 1946 to encourage observation and study of birds at sea by Naval and Royal Marine personnel, the society has opened its membership to all birdwatchers who share its interests. Members include many from the merchant navy, ocean weatherships, the offshore oil industry, yachtsmen and passengers on cruise-liners. The society is affiliated to the British Trust for Ornithology and the International Council for Bird Preservation (British Section). It has developed a reporting system using standardised recording forms and census sheets for seabird and landbird reports. It publishes two bulletins a year plus the annual journal *Sea Swallow*.

The Seabird Group
(Secretary: Dr P.J. Ewins, NCC, Archway house, 7 Eastcheap, Letchworth, Herts SG6 3DG). Maintains a directory of members interests, including census work on breeding seabirds, and investigates the distribution of birds at sea. *Seabird Group Newsletter* published quarterly, *Seabird* annually.

IN THE USA . . .

American Birding Association
PO Box 4335 Austin, Texas 78765.
National Audubon Society
950 Third Avenue, New York NY10022.

IN CANADA . . .
Canadian Nature Foundation
75 Albert Street, Ottawa K1P 6G1

IN AUSTRALIA. . . .
Australian Bird Study Association
PO Box A313, Sydney South NSW 2000.
Bird Observers Club
PO Box 185, 183 Springvale Road, Nunawading, Victoria 3131.
Royal Australian Ornithologists Union
21 Gladstone St Moonee Ponds, Victoria 3039.

IN NEW ZEALAND . . .
Ornithological Society of New Zealand
c/o Dominion Museum, Wellington.
Royal Forest and Bird Preservation Society of New Zealand
PO Box 631, Wellington.

SCIENTIFIC NAMES
(of species mentioned in the main text)

Albatross
Black-browed — *Diomedea melanophris*
Black-footed — *D. nigripes*
Buller's — *D. bulleri*
Laysan — *D. immutabilis*
Royal — *D. epomophora*
Short-tailed — *D. albatrus*
Wandering — *D. exulans*
Waved — *D. irrorata*
Yellow-nosed — *D. chlororhynchos*

Auk
Little — *Alle alle*

Auklet
Cassin's — *Ptychoramphus aleuticus*

Crested — *Aethia cristatella*
Rhinoceros — *Cerorhinca monocerata*

Avocet
American — *Recurvirostra americana*

Pied — *Avocetta recurvirostra*

Booby
Blue-footed — *Sula nebouxii*
Brown — *S. leucogaster*
Masked — *S. dactylatra*
Peruvian — *S. variegata*
Red-footed — *S. sula*

Bunting
Cretzschmars — *Emberiza caesia*

Cormorant
Cape — *Phalacrocorax capensis*
Double-crested — *P. auritus*
Great — *P. carbo*
Japanese — *P. capillatus*
Guanay — *P. bougainvillii*
Olivaceous — *P. olivaceus*
Pelagic — *P. pelagicus*
Pied — *P. varius*

Dolphin
Long-beaked spinner — *Stenella longirotris*

Dove
Turtle — *Streptopelia turtur*

Drongo
Crow-billed — *Dicrurus annectans*

Eagle
Steppe — *Aquila nipalensis*
White-tailed — *Haliaeetus albicilla*

Eider — *Somateria mollissima*

Falcon
Eleonora's — *Falco eleonorae*

Flamingo
Greater — *Phoenicopterus ruber*

Frigatebird
Ascension — *Fregata aquila*
Great — *F. minor*
Lesser — *F. ariel*
Magnificent — *F. magnificens*

Flycatcher
Black Paradise — *Terpsiphone corvina*

Fulmar
Northern — *Fulmarus glacialis*

Gannet
Australasian — *Sula serrator*
Cape — *S. capensis*
Northern — *S. bassana*

Grackle
Great-tailed — *Quiscanus mexicanus*

Gull
Audouin's — *Larus audouinnii*
Black-headed — *L. ridibundus*
Black-tailed — *L. crassirostris*
Brown-hooded — *L. maculipennis*
Bonaparte's — *L. philadelphia*
Californian — *L. californicus*
Chinese
  Black-headed — *L. saundersi*
Dolphin — *L. scoresbii*
Franklin's — *L. pipixcan*
Glaucous — *L. hyperboreus*
Glaucous-winged — *L. glaucescens*
Great Black-backed — *L. marinus*
Great Black-headed — *L. ichthyaetus*

201

Heermann's	*L. heermanni*
Herring	*L. argentatus*
Iceland	*L. glaucoides*
Indian Black-headed	*L. brunnicephalus*
Ivory	*L. pagophilia eburnea*
Kelp	*L. dominicanus*
Laughing	*L. atricilla*
Lesser Black-backed	*L. fuscus*
Mediterranean	*L. melanocephalus*
Mew	*L. canus*
Ring-billed	*L. delawarensis*
Ross's	*Rhodostethia rosea*
Sabine's	*Larus sabini*
Silver	*L. novaehollandiae*
Slaty-backed	*L. schistisagus*
Slender-billed	*L. genei*
Sooty	*L. hemprichi*
Western	*L. occidentalis*
White-eyed	*L. leucophthalmus*
Yellow-legged	*L.a. cachinnans*

Guillemot *Uria aalga*
Black *Cepphus grylle*
Brunnich's *Uria lomvia*
Pigeon *Cepphus columba*
Heron
Goliath *Ardea goliath*
Squacco *Ardeola ralloides*
Ibis
Sacred *Threskiornis aethiopicus*
Kestrel *Falco tinnunculus*
Kingfisher
Belted *Ceryle alcyon*
Pied *C. rudis*
Kiskadee
Great *Pitangus sulphuratus*
Kittiwake
Black-legged *Larus tridactyla*
Krill
Lobster *Munida gregaria*
Martin
Purple *Progne subis*
Merganser
Red-breasted *Mergus serrator*

Murrelet
Ancient *Synthliboramphus antiquum*
Marbled *Brachyramphus marmoratus*
Nightingale *Luscinia megarhynchas*
Noddy
Brown *Anous stolidus*
Black *A. tenuirostris minutus*
Osprey *Pandion haliaetus*
Pelican
Australian *Pelecanus conspicillatus*
American White *P. erythrorhynchos*
Brown *P. occidentalis*
Peruvian *P. (occidentalis) thagus*
Pink-backed *P. refescens*
Penguin
Adélie *Pygoscelis adeliae*
Emperor *Aptenodytes forsteri*
Gentoo *Pygoscelis papua*
King *Aptenodytes patagonicus*
Little *Eudyptes chrysolophus*
Magellanic *Spheniscus magellanicus*
Rockhopper *Eudyptes chrysostome*
Petrel
Bulwer's *Bulweria bulwerii*
Cape *Daption capense*
Great-winged *Pterodroma macroptera*
Soft-plumaged *P. mollis*
Southern Giant *Macronectes giganteus*
Phalarope
Red *Phalaropus fulicarius*
Red-necked *P. lobatus*
Wilson's *P. tricolour*
Plover
Spur-winged *Holopterus spinosus*
Prion
Fairy *Pachyptila turtur*
Puffin
Atlantic *Fratercula arctica*
Horned *F. corniculata*
Tufted *Lunda cirrhata*
Razorbill *Alca torda*

Robin	*Erithacus rubecula*
Scoter	
Black	*Melanitta nigra*
Surf	*M. perspicillata*
White-winged	*M. fusca*
Shag	
Imperial	*Phalacrocorax atriceps*
Shark	
Common	
Hammerhead	*Sphyrna zygaena*
Shearwater	
Audubon's	*Puffinus icherminieri*
Cory's	*Calonectris diomedea*
Flesh-footed	*Puffinus carneipes*
Fluttering	*P. gavia*
Great	*P. gravis*
Manx	*P. puffinus*
Short-tailed	*P. tenuirostris*
Sooty	*P. griseus*
Streaked	*Calonectris leucomelas*
Sheathbill	
American	*Chionis alba*
White-chinned	*Procellaria aequinoctialis*
Skimmer	
Black	*Rhynchops niger*
Skua	
Arctic	*Stercorarius parasiticus*
Great	*Catharacta skua*
Long-tailed	*Stercorarius longicaudus*
Pomarine	*S. pomarine*
Squid	
Flying	*Onchoteuthis banskii*
Stork	
Abdim's	*Ciconia abdimii*
Storm-Petrel	
European	*Hydrobates pelagicus*
Fork-tailed	*Oceanodroma furcata*
Leach's	*O. leucorhoa*
Madeiran	*O. castro*
White-bellied	*Fregetta gallaria*
White-faced	*Pelagodroma marina*
Wilson's	*Oceanites oceanicus*

Swallow	
Barn	*Hirundo rustica*
Mangrove	*Tachycineta albilinea*
Rough-winged	*Stelgidopteryx reficollis*
Swift	
Alpine	*Apus melba*
Common	*A. apus*
Tern	
Arctic	*Sterna paradisea*
Black-naped	*S. sumatrana*
Bridled	*S. anaethetus*
Cayenne	*S. (sandvicensis) eurygnatha*
Common	*S. hirundo*
Crested	*S. bergii*
Elegant	*S. elegans*
Forster's	*S. forsteri*
Gull-billed	*S. nilotica*
Inca	*Larosterna inca*
Lesser-crested	*Sterna bengalensis*
Roseate	*S. dougalli*
Royal	*S. maxima*
Sandwich	*S. sandvicensis*
Sooty	*S. fuscata*
Whiskered	*Chilidonias hybridus*
White	*Gygis alba*
White-fronted	*Sterna striata*
Tree	
Fig, weeping	*Ficus Benjamini*
Umbrella	*Schofflera actiniphylla*
Tropicbird	
Red-billed	*Phaethon aethereus*
Red-tailed	*P. rubricauda*
White-tailed	*P. lepturus*
Vulture	
Black	*Coragypa atratus*
Turkey	*Cathartes aura*
Warbler	
Blackcap	*Sylvia atricapilla*
Spectacled	*Sylvia conspicillata*
Subalpine	*S. cantillans*
Willow	*Phylloscopus trochilus*
Whitethroat	
Lesser	*Sylvia curruca*

ACKNOWLEDGEMENTS

Ronald Lockley first channelled my enthusiasm for small boats into a desire to land on every beach and explore every cliff and cave in sight, and I warmly recognise his influence. John Sparks, as Head of the BBC's Natural History Unit, happily sent me to visit far-off islands, but it was Lady Phillipa and Sir Peter Scott who first opened the magic door and took me to the enchanted Galapagos Islands, living on a diet of rice and fried eggs with the Ecuadorean Navy but seeing a glimpse of paradise.

My grateful thanks to all the intrepid souls who have sailed on our bird cruises both at home and to distant places, and most especially to the captains and crews of the legendary P&O fleet and to Commander Casement of the Royal Naval Birdwatching Society. Sonia Lindblad, Colin Cooper, Fred Hitchin and David Dingle found me various berths as ship's naturalist, and even let my family travel as well. Special thanks to P&O's ornithological mole, Bob Burridge, whose cover as a cabin steward has allowed him to bird the seven seas, to the great benefit of all who have enjoyed his company. I also acknowledge with gratitude the help of the Kingsbridge branch of Devon County Library.

And lastly, thanks to Elizabeth and Bernard Watts for their help in checking the proofs but mostly for their stimulating company.

TS
February 1989
Kingsbridge, Devon

Cape Petrel

INDEX